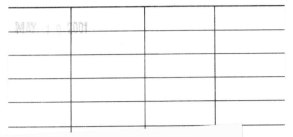

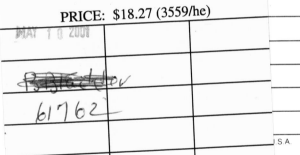

Cadillac of Destroyers

Dedicated to:
Robert W. Barrie RCNVR & RCN 1943 - 1963

CADILLAC

OF DESTROYERS

HMCS *St. Laurent* and Her Successors

Ron Barrie and Ken Macpherson

Vanwell Publishing Limited
St. Catharines, ON

Vanwell Publishing Limited
1 Northrup Crescent
St. Catharines, ON L2R 7S2

Printed in Canada
99 98 97 96   1 2 3 4 5

Canadian Cataloguing in Publication Data
Barrie, Ron, 1949-
    Cadillac of Destroyers

Includes bibliographical references and index.
ISBN 1-55125-036-5
1. Destroyers (Warships) - Canada - History - 20th century.
2. Destroyer escorts - Canada - History - 20th century.
I. Macpherson, Ken. II. Title.

V825.5.C3b37 1996   359.8'354'0971   C96-931632-1

CONTENTS

FOREWORD

Following the successful conclusion of World War 2 and the immediate demobilization of "wartime only" personnel from the services, the Canadian government was faced with the problem of deciding what Canada would require in size and tasks for the permanent military forces, both nationally and internationally.

The past six years had seen our country come of age, with the well-earned recognition by the Allies that in the postwar years, Canada's influence in the maintenance of world peace would be expected and relied upon. Thus, a return to the small prewar strength of the RCN was not contemplated, and necessary support facilities as well as ships would be required.

The key questions were, what size? What tasks?

The first postwar authorization was for 10,000 personnel, a balanced force of aircraft carriers, cruisers and destroyers, and a Reserve fleet.

Within two years, however, the government shifted priorities and returned to its short-sighted prewar views, cutting the defence budget by 25 percent. This resulted in the RCN being reduced to 7,500 personnel and a smaller fleet consisting of one aircraft carrier, one cruiser and five destroyers.

The outbreak of the Korean War in 1950 brought about a complete change again, the government now approving a naval force of 20,000 personnel and a role-change to concentrate on anti-submarine warfare. The Naval Board, appreciating the need for a Canadian-designed and produced anti-submarine destroyer, approved the design of the St. Laurent class. As a consequence, twenty ships were commissioned in the decade after 1955.

This bold and futuristic decision by the Board recognized that within Canada we had the necessary knowledge, experience and talent to facilitate the success of the program.

Follow-on designs resulted in the General Purpose class (not built), the Iroquois class and the recent Halifax class.

Today, unfortunately, we see again a complete negation of the requirement for a well-trained, balanced capability within the three services. History has revealed repeatedly the difficulty and expense incurred when our country is called upon in the name of international organizations to resist a determined and well equipped aggressor.

In this book the authors have prepared a balanced review of RCN construction programs from 1950, which will be welcomed by naval historians and readers.

Robert W. Timbrell, CMM, DSC, CD
Rear Admiral, Royal Canadian Navy (Rtd).
RADM Timbrell was the first commanding officer,
1955-57, of HMCS St. Laurent.

PREFACE

HMCS *St. Laurent* was the first warship designed and built entirely in Canada. A startling ship when she entered service in the fall of 1955, she created a stir among naval circles in Britain and Washington when it was realized that Canada had stolen a march on those two great navies, and got her first postwar destroyers up and running.

St. Laurent and her sisters became the Navy's prime providers of seagoing experience, and showed Canada's flag proudly in most of the major ports of the world. Only four of the original twenty are still in commission, but the "Cadillacs" (as they came to be nick-named) will be remembered with affection by the thousands of officers, men, women, reservists and cadets who served in them.

It was our purpose to set forth a description of the design requirements, original specifications, and modifications made to *St. Laurent* class destroyer escorts and later classes derived from them. Also included are the *Iroquois* class and the new *Canadian Patrol Frigates*. Each of the ships is illustrated, and in the case of ships radically altered by rebuilding, the enthusiast will find "before and after" photographs to illustrate those changes.

We have examined the DELEX and TRUMP programmes in some detail, as well as providing a summary of each ship's history, garnered from the often skimpy published material available.

Even in selecting a title, we were faced with a problem in that the classification of fighting ships has undergone confusing changes since World War 2. It is no longer possible to compare weaponry, but in terms of displacement our destroyer escorts compare with a large destroyer of fifty years ago, and our new frigates bear no kinship whatever to those of WW2, being of a tonnage comparable to that of a WW1 light cruiser!

We have done our best in this respect, and trust that our readers will understand. Any errors or omissions are the authors', and comments will be welcomed.

Ron Barrie & Ken Macpherson
March 1996

Three DDEs in various stages of fitting-out at Canadian Vickers Ltd. about 1955. They are probably, from right to left, *ASSINIBOINE, OTTAWA, AND ST. LAURENT*. The nearest one had not yet had her anchor-recess opening cut out, while the other two are having the doors fitted.

Design Requirements and Construction

ST. LAURENT CLASS

In November 1948, the Canadian government announced its intention to build seven escort vessels. These vessels were to specialize in anti-submarine warfare—a role to which Canada had devoted herself during World War 2.

The new ships were to be of destroyer size, with a speed in excess of 25 knots, and capable of carrying the latest in sophisticated electronic detection gear. Designed in Canada under the direction of Constructor Captain Rowland Baker, RN, (loaned from the Royal Corps of Naval Constructors) the ships could be rapidly produced in time of crisis. Emphasis was stressed on seakeeping, noise/weight reduction and nuclear, biological and chemical (NBC) protection.

Innovative ideas were also introduced with these ships: omission of superfluous fittings and scuttles on a sleek, rounded hull designed for seakeeping ability and to counter the formation of ice; acoustic insulation; weight-saving use of aluminum in the superstructure, funnel casing, masts, storerooms, magazines and furniture. To further assist in the reduction of ice build-up, the anchors were stored in recesses behind *heated*, manually operated doors, and the capstan was to be located under the forecastle

ST. LAURENT on 17 October, 1955, on final trials before her commissioning later that month—a superb view of this then-novel ship.

9

SASKATCHEWAN'S after 3"/50 gun, with its radar director between the barrels.

cleaning. This class was the first designed so that it was possible to pass from bow to stern without going onto the upper deck.

These ships also introduced another radical concept. An "operations room" was to be put down one deck and abaft the bridge. This was where the captain would fight the ship. When the design team presented this idea to the Naval Board of the day, some resistance was encountered, as its members were uncomfortable with the idea of the captain conning the ship other than from the bridge.

The Naval Board decided to try out this concept in HMCS *Algonquin*, which was accordingly modernized from the deck up. Part of this modernization included an enclosed bridge with an operations room behind. The concept proved successful, and the *St. Laurent* class were among the first ships to incorporate this feature.

Two 3"/50 calibre, twin gun mounts, forward and aft, were installed as main armament. Primarily to be used against air threats, these guns provided a weak capability against surface targets. Also included were two single 40mm Bofors guns, sited to port and starboard on the after superstructure. Two of the latest anti-submarine triple-barrelled mortars, the Limbo Mk.NC 10 (from Britain) were fitted. These mortars could be directed by sonar fire control systems or operated manually. Launchers for homing torpedoes were also installed, somewhat reminiscent of WW2 depth charge throwers but angled downward so that the torpedoes would enter the water nose-first. The torpedo's guidance system enabled it to alter course in pursuit of a target taking evasive action.

deck. The ships were designed so that operating, living and working areas could be sealed off from the outside environment, thereby permitting operation in an NBC environment. Fire-resistant paint was used throughout the ship. Also included was the fitting of a pre-wetting system, which would permit the washing off of any contamination that might be encountered. For the first time, air-conditioning (the only scuttles and windows were located in the bridge superstructure, and the bridge windows were heated) was installed.

The ships were designed with all modern conveniences for the crew. This included bunks (the first to be fitted in RCN ships as built), larger storage areas for personal gear, a central galley system and such features as showers with "rounded" corners to facilitate

The latest sonar, (See "Conversion" section) also from Britain and modified to suit Canadian purposes, was installed. State-of-the-art radar from the U.S., again modified for Canadian use, was introduced.

The propulsion system was a compact, twin-boiler design driving two shafts. Cruising turbines were to take the ships up to 20 knots, when the main turbines would kick in and boost the ship up to 28 knots. This was to be achieved through what was called a "Napier" clutch, which was fitted in the *St. Laurent* and worked extremely well. However, the Royal Navy had installed the same system in HMS *Whitby* at about this time for tests, and *Whitby* suffered an explosion of the clutch which killed a number of her crew. As a result of this incident, *St. Laurent* returned to the old system of engine throttles.

Except experimentally, this was the first time in the Commonwealth or the United States in which hardened and ground gearing was used in the engines. The weight and size of the housing was thereby greatly reduced. The boiler room was not pressurized, and therefore could be sealed off from contamination. The ships were fitted with twin rudders, providing a high degree of manoeuverability.

Described as an "electrical wonderland", *St. Laurent* and her sisters had electronic and electrical systems more extensive and complex than World War 2 ships twice her size. Everything was dependent on electrical power: armament, navigation, cooking, ventilation, air conditioning, and communications. Another first for a Canadian ship—440-volt alternating current was installed. Over 50 miles of electric cable were used in her construction. Some 330 motors and generators were installed, providing power for a wide variety of equipment. The ships were equipped with five generators producing 1,400 kilowatts.

St. Laurent was fitted with 12 separate telephone systems for internal communications. Specialized lines were used for such things as docking ship, damage control, radar maintenance and fuelling at sea. A remote-control system made it possible to broadcast or receive orders from any of 30 positions throughout the ship.

She was equipped with three radio rooms capable of transmitting and receiving on low, medium, very high and ultra-high frequencies. A fourth was equipped with direction-finding equipment. A specialized message centre was equipped with teletype and a cryptographic room with coding devices.

Radar systems for gunnery fire control, navigation, surface warning, air warning and airborne early warning were fitted, as was sonar of the latest design.

The ships were built using an innovative technique known as "unit construction", the hull and main components being designed so that they could be built in units. Ranging in weight from five to twenty-six tons, each was built separately, then carried to the building ways where it was positioned for final welding to the hull. Thus the hull grew by the addition of a complete section, rather than a plate or rib at a time. It was expected that in an emergency, structural steel manufacturers across the country could be given specific sections for prefabrication. These sections could then be transported via rail, each section being designed to be able to go through any rail tunnel across Canada. This would then reduce the building time at the shipyard.

The ships were to be totally supported from Canadian resources, which brought an economic windfall in contracts to Canadian industry.

These seven ships, the *St. Laurent* class, came to be known in Canadian circles as the "Cadillac of Destroyers", so radically advanced and luxurious were they by comparison with the destroyers of WW2.

The *St. Laurent* programme was to be completed by June 30, 1954, however delays were encountered in the procurement of steel, component parts and machine tools from other countries. All seven of the class were completed by 1957.

RESTIGOUCHE AND *MACKENZIE* CLASSES

On 4 June, 1951, an additional seven anti-submarine ships were ordered. These were to become the *Restigouche* class, and all were completed by 1959.

Initially it had been estimated that each ship would cost $8 million to build, however this estimate soon grew to $15 million, and in the end ranged between $23 and $25 million for the *St. Laurent* and *Restigouche* classes. By the time the *Mackenzie* class was completed, the cost per ship had reached $28 million.

After investigating the possibility of a cheaper vessel, it was decided to build another six ships of similar design to the *Restigouche* class. Sometimes referred to as the *Repeat Restigouche* class, the six ships actually ended up as two classes, the first four forming the *Mackenzie* class and the last two the *Annapolis* class.

The contract for the first *Mackenzie* class vessel was let in 1958 and the order completed in 1963.

CONVERSION

The two major deficiencies in these ships were not the fault of the designers.

The ships lacked long-range sonar (the sonar installed had the same range as the World War 2 type—2000 yards). This shortcoming was overcome with the development of the Canadian-designed and produced AN/SQS 500 series Variable Depth Sonar (VDS). VDS was being worked upon as early as the late 1940s, but an operable system was not available until the early 60s.

The second major shortcoming became apparent with the development of the nuclear submarine, which could travel submerged at speeds far exceeding that of our surface vessels. With the marriage of the Sea King helicopter to the destroyer, this problem would be to a large extent overcome.

The concept of a helicopter operating from a destroyer-sized vessel was not new. It had been suggested during WW2, but the technology was not available and the idea was shelved. During the Korean conflict of the early 1950s, the helicopter proved its usefulness in a variety of functions over land. By 1955 the RCN had formed an anti-submarine squadron of helicopters operating from the aircraft carrier *Magnificent*.

During the summer of 1956 *St. Laurent* conducted trials of a helicopter operating from a destroyer. The first landings were made on the forecastle of the ship, in order to allow those on the bridge to observe proceedings. Then the Limbo well coverings were strengthened and landings and take-offs conducted from the quarterdeck.

This led to the installation of a more permanent flight deck on board the *Prestonian* class frigate *Buckingham,* October to December 1956, then in the destroyer escort *Ottawa* in 1957. These trials proved the practicality of operating a helicopter from a small ship. Room was made for a hangar from which to carry out maintenance and provide shelter for the helicopter, thus extending its operational life. Finally a system for hauling down the helicopter to the deck and winching it into the hangar was devised. Officially known as the Helicopter Haul-Down and Rapid Securing Device, it is known in Canadian naval circles as the "Beartrap", and makes it possible to land a heavy helicopter in all types of weather and almost any sea state. This clever Canadian device has been adopted by other countries world-wide. In June 1962 *Assiniboine* was taken in hand to be fitted with the Canadian-designed Variable Depth Sonar and a helicopter hangar and landing deck.

In order to accomplish this conversion, the ship was stripped and gutted except for the main machinery spaces and some of the forward sections. Messing accommodation was made roomier and office facilities rearranged. The recreation area forward was enlarged and fitted with better facilities. The hull was strengthened for the hangar and helicopter deck, as well as the fuelling facilities required for the helicopter. The stern was radically reconfigured for the installation of the VDS and its associated equipment.

SASKATCHEWAN'S ASROC launcher.

Activated fin stabilizers were added to reduce roll in rough weather as an aid to helicopter operations. The ship emerged with two funnels located athwartship, in order to accommodate the hangar. The after 3"/50 calibre gun and one of the Limbo mortars were removed in order to make room for the helicopter facilities. In sum, these alterations were to cost $24 million per ship.

In the early 1960s it was planned to refurbish the *Restigouche* class with new equipment to further enhance their ASW capabilities, but by 1968 economic strictures allowed only four of the ships to be reconfigured into what came to be referred to as the *Improved Restigouche (IRE)* class. This entailed the installation of an ASROC (Anti-Submarine Rocket) launcher and magazine. Simply put, the ASROC is a rocket-propelled anti-submarine homing torpedo, the rocket carrying the torpedo approximately six miles from the ship before entering the water. Also fitted were the 257 Anti-Submarine Warfare Data System and the Canadian-designed AN/SQS-505 variable depth and hull-mounted sonar systems as well as new communications gear and other electronic equipment. This necessitated the installation of a taller,

lattice mast. The program was completed between 1967 and 1972.

Construction had not yet started on the *Annapolis* and *Nipigon* (the last two of the 20 ships built), before the conversion program was started on the *St. Laurent* class, and so it was decided to build the final two from the keel up with helicopter facilities and VDS.

In November 1981, all 16 Canadian destroyers were taken out of service during the winter owing to cracks discovered in the superheater headers of the *Ottawa*. All of the ships were checked and *Assiniboine*, *Margaree*, *Saguenay*, *Skeena*, *Kootenay* and *Terra Nova* discovered to have similar cracks. Within six months, all were repaired and back in service.

With the decommissioning of HMCS *Kootenay* on 18 December, 1995, only four of the original twenty remained - two of the *IRE* class and the two *Annapolis* class. Soon, they too will be making their final sail-past.

IROQUOIS CLASS DESTROYERS

This programme was announced by the government on 22 December, 1964. It was an advancement on the DDH programme, the ships to have space for two helicopters, a surface-to-air missile system, new sonar and a heavy (5-inch) gun. Although specializing in ASW, the ships were envisioned as being much more "general purpose" in nature, capable of being more flexibly employed than previous destroyers. In fact, the hull design was based on that of the never-built "General Purpose Frigates" of the early 1960s.

The contract cost was $192.7 million for four ships, but owing to design changes and a revised contracting system, the cost rose to $252 million (or $62.5 million per ship). This would appear to support the view, held in certain quarters, that it is impractical to design and build a new class of only four ships.

These ships were the first in the world to be all gas turbine-powered, and the first Canadian ships to be equipped with a point

The 5-inch gun as originally fitted in the *Iroquois* class.

defence missile system - the Sea Sparrow. These surface-to-air missiles were sited in a deckhouse forward of the bridge, stored horizontally across the beam. For firing, the launching arm extended out from the deckhouse to port and starboard. When on the launchers, the missiles could be fired within 33 seconds from initial warm-up to extended position. Reload time was one and one-half to two minutes.

This class of destroyers was equipped with flume type anti-rolling tanks to stabilize the ships at low speed, a pre-wetting system to counter radioactive fallout, an enclosed citadel, and bridge control of machinery.

The gas turbines feed through a Swiss double-reduction gearbox to two five-bladed, controllable-pitch propellers. With this system, it was reported that the ships could change direction from 29 knots ahead to astern movement in 46 seconds, and could stop from full speed ahead within 750 feet!

In June of 1983 the government announced the Tribal Update and Modernization Programme *(TRUMP)*. This programme would

IROQUOIS as she originally appeared in 1972.

change the ships to "area air defence" ships, while retaining strong anti-submarine capabilities. All of the work was to be done by the Davie Shipbuilding Company, Lauzon, and be completed by 1992 at a cost of $650 million.

The TRUMPed ships show significant improvements in all aspects of their operational capability. New surveillance and detection systems include long- and medium-range radars integrated through an automated radar track management system. As well, new navigational radars were installed.

New weapons include Plessy Shield Chaff and infra-red decoy launchers as well as a Nixie torpedo decoy system. An OTO Melara 76mm super rapid-fire gun, an automatic Phalanx Block 1 close-in weapon system, new fire control radars and a weapons direction system were also fitted. The centrepiece of the TRUMP project is the Standard Missile Block 3 surface-to-air missile in a vertical launch system (VLS). All the new combat equipment will be controlled and co-ordinated using SHINCOM (Ship Integrated Communications) and state-of-the-art command and control system.

Other TRUMP features include an improved propulsion system with the installation of the new Allison gas turbine cruise engines through improvements made to the main gearing coupled to new variable pitch propellers. A SHINMACS (Ship Integrated Machinery Control System) allows direct control of all machinery from the bridge or the machinery control room. A water-displaced fuel system has been incorporated to compensate for the 350 tons of top-weight TRUMP has added to the 280-class destroyers. This system is expected to improve the ships' "slow roll" problems. As well, the existing anti-submarine warfare suite has been augmented with a new sonobuoy processor and an enhanced torpedo-handling arrangement.

Other improvements included hull strengthening, an infrared suppression device in the (now) single funnel, fire detection and suppression systems and upgrading of living spaces.

All four ships were expected to be fully operational by the end of 1995. The refit, whose cost totalled $1.8 billion, is expected to give Canada another 20 years of service from this class of ships.

CANADIAN PATROL FRIGATES, CITY CLASS

On July 29, 1983, a contract for $3.85 billion was awarded to Saint John Shipbuilding and Drydock Co. Ltd. (SJSL), as the prime contractor responsible for the building of six *Halifax* class patrol frigates. Sub-contractors were Versatile Vickers Industries Group (VVI) who, owing to lack of facilities, sub-contracted the construction of three frigates to Marine Industries Limited (MIL), Sorel. PARAMAX Electronics was awarded the job of obtaining, integrating and installing the various weapons, communications and sensor equipment to be used in the frigates. To date, this has been the largest and most complex project in Canadian military history.

On 29 December, 1987, the order was expanded to include a further six frigates, referred to as the *Montreal* class. It was expected that these ships would be 32 feet (10 metres) longer, to accommodate messing arrangements for a mixed-gender crew, but this plan failed to materialize (owing to financial constraints), and the *Montreal* class are exact duplicates (externally) of the *Halifax* class.

Internally, however, a hydraulic starter system for the gas turbine and an electronic reverse-osmosis water evaporation system (instead of the noisier steam-driven system) are being fitted in the *Montreal* class. A more powerful computer for the combat system (more memory) was also included in the Batch 2 frigates. This type of computer is expected to be retrofitted into the *Halifax* class. In 1986, the first steel was cut for the first frigate, HMCS *Halifax*. These all-steel ships have been built using a modular construction technique. Initially, it was thought to build 56 of these modular units, and join them together into 26 erection units, which would then be assembled to form the ship. After the first three ships were built at SJSL in this manner, it was found easier to construct nine mega-modules instead. The six ships of the *Montreal* Batch were built using this latter method.

These low-silhouetted ships were designed to have a minimal radar signature. Low infrared features were incorporated into the design to reduce their attraction to heat-seeking missiles and, like earlier Canadian destroyers, the ships can seal themselves against biological and chemical attack. The fully automated bridge, sited well forward on the hull, offers 300 degrees of visibility.

The two gas turbines driving these twin-screwed ships, as well as the three gearboxes used, are mounted on "rafts" which are affixed to the ship using rubber. The diesel engine is "double-mounted" on rubber, and flexible couplings are used from the gearbox, all in an effort to reduce noise emanating from the ship. The ships have one large rudder.

DELEX
(Destroyer Life Extension Programme)

Started in 1979, this programme was implemented to extend the life of Canada's 16 steam-driven destroyers by 8 to 12 years beyond the normally anticipated 25 years. It extended the life of the *St. Laurent* class and improved the capabilities of the *Improved Restigouche, Mackenzie* and *Annapolis* classes. Each ship was expected to complete this programme within ten months. The programme could be summed up as having three main objectives:

a) Provision and installation of equipment and the carrying out of "one time only" repairs necessary to ensure safe operation of the destroyers beyond 30 years.

b) Provision and installation of equipment to maintain a minimum level of combat capability in the *Annapolis* and *Improved Restigouche* classes.

c) To maintain minimum sonar capability and communications inter-operability in the *Mackenzie* class.

In order to accomplish these objectives, general major improvements were made in the following areas:
Replacement of three radar systems
Modernization of fire control systems
Replacement of electronic warfare systems
Replacement of command, control and navigational systems
Replacement of sonar systems
Replacement of message-handling systems

In actual application to the ships, the program was broken down into two parts which, as the ships were brought in for refit, were interwoven. The basic DELEX addressed the hull and machinery. In all classes, as many as possible of the auxiliary machinery units were replaced, and pieces that were not replaced, were thoroughly overhauled. Full DELEX included the other major improvements mentioned above.

The six ships of *St. Laurent* class were given enough modernization to enable them to remain operational into the late 1980s. This involved hull and machinery repairs sufficient to take them to sea in safety.

For the *Improved Restigouche* class, the DELEXing included the installation of an ADLIPS tactical data system, the fitting of a Mk.127E navigational radar, SPS-502 radar, and AN/SPG-515 fire control radar to the Mk.69 gunnery control system. A TACAN antenna was fitted on a pole mast replacing the top part of the lattice mast. The 103mm Bofors illumination rocket rails were removed and a Super RBOC chaff system fitted instead. Two Mk.32 triple torpedo tubes were added between the ASROC launcher and the Limbo well. The C3 dome was fared into the hull lines in the permanently-down position. This increased the draft of the vessels by almost four feet. New communications equipment was installed, including a new message-handling system.

All of the *Mackenzie* class destroyers were DELEXed at Esquimalt by Burrard/Yarrows Inc., 1982-85. The Mk.NC 10 torpedo launchers were removed and replaced by two triple torpedo tubes sited on the quarterdeck. These new tubes make use of the Mk.46 torpedo. An AN/SQS-505 C3 sonar dome was

SHIPS' PARTICULARS / ST. LAURENT CLASS					
Statistical Data					
Name	Pendant	Laid Down	Launched	Commissioned	Paid Off
ASSINIBOINE	234	19/5/52	12/2/54	16/8/56	14/12/88
FRASER	233	11/12/51	19/2/53	28/6/57	5/10/94
MARGAREE	230	12/9/51	29/3/56	5/10/57	2/5/92
OTTAWA	229	8/6/51	29/4/53	10/11/56	31/7/92
SAGUENAY	206	4/4/51	30/7/53	15/12/56	26/6/90
SKEENA	207	1/6/51	19/8/52	30/3/57	1/11/93
ST. LAURENT	205	24/11/50	30/11/51	29/10/55	14/6/74

N.B. Owing to the unit construction technique used in the building of these vessels, work on hull units started before components were laid on the slips. "Laid down" dates are thus actually when work commenced,

Displacement (as built):	2,263 tons standard, 2,800 tons full load	
(as DDH):	2,263 tons standard, 3,051 tons full load	
Dimensions:	366' x 42' x 13'2"	
Speed:	Cruising - 14 knots	
	Maximum - 28 knots	
Endurance:	4,570 n/m at 12 knots	
Machinery:	Geared turbines - 2 shafts, 2 propellers,	
	SHP: 30,000	
Boilers:	2 Babcock & Wilcox water tube	
Crew:	12 officers, 237 men	

Armament (as built): 4-3"/50 calibre Mk.33 (two twin mounts): dual purpose mounts, 85° elevation, 50 rounds per minute to 7.9 miles; 2-40mm (two single mounts)*; 2 Mk.NC 10 Limbo triple-barrelled, automatic-loading mortars, range 3280'. Homing torpedoes.

(as DDH): 2-3"(one twin mount - details above) 1 triple-barrelled Limbo Mk.NC 10 Mortar; 6-21" Mk.32 (2 triple-barrelled) torpedo tubes, anti-submarine active/passive to 6.8 miles at 40 knots; 1 CH-124 Sea King ASW Helicopter

ASSININBOINE, OTTAWA, SKEENA and *ST. LAURENT* were fitted with these two mounts. The other three were not, as it was determined that the two 3"/50s could respond in most anticipated situations.

installed on the hull, new communications equipment fitted, and certain modifications made to the SPS-12 air search radar.

The two ships of the *Annapolis* class had a more complex DELEXing refit done, so much more detailed that it is sometimes referred to as "DELEX/265 Conversion" programme. The *Improved Restigouche*-type mast was fitted and mounted with, among other radars, the AN/SPS-503 radar. The vacuum-tubed AN/SPS-10 radar was replaced with the solid state AN/SPS-10D gear, which uses the same antenna. Below the waterline, the antiquated AN/SQS-502, 503 and SQS-10/11 sonar sets were replaced by the AN/SQS-505(V) sonar in a fixed, fared dome. The operations room was restructured and fitted with two ADLIPS units, thereby

increasing the ships' capabilities to process information and allowing them to share this information with ships of other NATO navies. *Nipigon* was utilized as the test bed for the AN/SQS-505(V) unit, sometimes referred to as a "smart" 505. A new underwater telephone system was installed and a Mk.60 gunnery control system fitted. The Limbo Mk.NC 10 mortar and the AN/SQR-504 variable depth sonar and associated equipment were removed and their place taken by the AN/SQR-19 CANTASS unit. Super RBOC systems were installed also.

ASSINIBOINE on 8 June, 1956, on trials shortly before she was commissioned

Assiniboine (2nd)

H MCS *Assiniboine* was built by Marine Industries Ltd. (MIL) Sorel, Quebec. The first ship delivered postwar to the RCN by that firm, she was commissioned at Sorel on 16 August, 1956.

She arrived in Halifax on 25 August of that year and took up duties with the Third Canadian Escort Squadron. She left for her first major deployment in early October, a goodwill cruise to Northern European ports with other ships of her squadron as well as ships from the First Canadian Escort Squadron. The ships returned to Halifax in mid-November.

In June 1957 *Assiniboine*, along with *Margaree*, participated at an International Naval Review at Hampton Roads, Virginia.

Transferred to the west coast in January 1959, *Assiniboine* became a member of the Second Canadian Escort Squadron. On 15-16 July of that year she played host to the Queen and Prince Philip on a trip from Vancouver to Nanaimo, B.C. Her next rendezvous with royalty would be in the summer of 1983, when she escorted HMY *Britannia* with Prince Charles and Princess Diana on board during a tour of the Maritime Provinces.

In June 1962, she was decommissioned for conversion to a helicopter-carrying destroyer (DDH), the first of the class to be so converted. The major part of the conversion was done by Victoria Machinery Depot Company, Victoria, B.C., with the work being completed by HMC Dockyard, Esquimalt.

Twenty-eight June, 1963, saw her recommissioned, and at the end of September she set sail for Halifax, arriving there on 26 October for service with Atlantic Command. With the installation of the "Beartrap" helicopter haul-down system, she became the trial ship for this equipment.

For the next two years, she sought out storms around the North Atlantic in order to test the "Beartrap" system. The trials were successful, although with a little less than 13 feet between the helicopter's rotor blades and the door of the hangar, it was close at times!

In January 1975, *Assiniboine* assisted in the rescue of crew members from the freighter *Barma,* which had begun shipping water about 185 miles off Boston.

On 23 April, 1979, she was decommissioned to begin her Destroyer Life Extension (DELEX) refit at Canadian Vickers Ltd., Montreal. Refurbished, she returned to service on 16 November of the same year.

An embarrassing incident occurred on 30 June, 1981, when she was leading four other ships of the Standing Naval Force Atlantic out of Halifax, and grounded on Point Pleasant Shoal.

While acting as an escort for the Tall Ships race from Bermuda to Halifax in the early summer of 1984, *Assiniboine* took a prominent role in the search for survivors when the British sailing vessel *Marques* went down. For this, *Assiniboine* was awarded the *Chief of Defence Staff Unit Commendation*, the second ship in the Navy to receive this award.

In July 1984, she returned to Halifax from southern exercises with fractures of her upper deck stringers and plating. This necessitated drydocking on 17 July, 1984, at MIL, Sorel, for what was expected to be a 10-month refit. Owing to a strike, however, she stayed there for 17 months.

During her career, *Assiniboine* logged more than 700,000 nautical miles, sailed in five oceans and visited every continent except Australia and Antarctica.

After 32 years of yeoman service, she was decommissioned on 14 December, 1988, and on 3 January, 1989 taken off the active Canadian Forces (CF) order of battle. She afterward served as a floating classroom for Fleet School technicians in Halifax until January, 1995, when she was turned over to Crown Assets for disposal.

Battle Honours:		
	Atlantic	1939-1945
	Biscay	1944
	English Channel	1944-1945

The Heritage: *The first* Assiniboine *was a destroyer, the former HMS* Kempenfelt. *She served in the RCN 1939-1945, and was wrecked on Prince Edward Island in 1945 en route for scrapping.*

ASSINIBOINE in 1971, as modified to a DDE. Her gun is turned aft to lessen damage from spray.

20

HMCS *Fraser* (2nd)

✪

H MCS *Fraser* is unusual in having been laid down and launched in one shipyard and completed by another. On 11 December, 1951, construction of the ship commenced at Burrard Dry Dock Company Limited, Vancouver, B.C. After being launched, she was taken to Yarrows Ltd, Esquimalt, and completed. The sixth of her class, she was commissioned at Yarrows on 28 June, 1957.

She joined the Second Destroyer Squadron at Esquimalt, and for the next eight years plied Pacific waters on patrol and training duties. During these years she visited such places as Singapore, Hong Kong, Vietnam, Pearl Harbour, Mexico and San Diego. On 13 November, 1960, she assisted the disabled yacht *Redwitch* toward San Diego, and in July 1964 towed the vessel *Yaqui Queen* into Mazatlan, Mexico. On 7 April, 1964, she consigned the ashes of Vice Admiral H.R.Reid to the sea, performing the same office for Rear-Admiral P. Tisdall on 23 March, 1965.

On 12 January, 1965, she left Esquimalt to participate in a blast test off the Hawaiian Island of Kahoolawe. On 6 February, along with USN warships, she was subjected to a first test and then returned to Esquimalt. On 16 April, she returned to the area to undergo another such test, easily withstanding both of them. These tests were designed as a means of assessing the RCN's nuclear defence capability.

Fraser then proceeded to Canadian Vickers Shipyard, Montreal, and upon arrival on 2 July, 1965, was decommissioned for conversion to a helicopter-carrying destroyer. The seventh and

FRASER in November 1961, off the California coast.

last of her class to be converted, she was recommissioned on 22 October, 1966 for service with the east coast fleet.

Her first landing of a Sea King took place on 15 June, 1967. Early that October, *Fraser* was alongside in Washington, D.C. to demonstrate Beartrap, the Canadian-designed helicopter haul-down system.

On 14-17 May, 1969, she represented Canada at the Spithead Review off Portsmouth for Queen Elizabeth II. During the summer of 1970, *Fraser* made her first Great Lakes cruise. This deployment saw her visit 10 cities, the farthest west being Duluth, Minnesota.

In May, 1973, *Fraser* entered Category "C" reserve, but was re-activated on 11 March, 1974. After undergoing most of a major refit at Davie Shipyard in Montreal, she returned to Halifax and dockyard hands for completion of the job before becoming an operational unit of the fleet once again that fall.

28 November, 1980 saw the ship participate in the rescue of twelve British seaman from the fishing vessel *St.Irene* off the coast of Holland. For her efforts, she was later awarded the *Chief of Defence Staff Unit Commendation*. She was the first ship to receive this particular award.

In December 1980, while operating with STANAVFORLANT, she remained in European waters over the Christmas holiday season in case the force should be required to respond to problems in Poland. *Fraser* completed her DELEX refit at Canadian Vickers Ltd., Montreal, between 19 October, 1981 and 28 May, 1982, subsequently becoming to all intents and purposes a "test" ship. In 1986 she was fitted experimentally with the towed passive detection array system known as ETASS, and conducted tests with this equipment for the following two years. This equipment was to become known, once the trials were completed, as the CANTASS gear.

In May 1987 she completed trials of the AN/SLQ-25 Nixie torpedo decoy system. This system would eventually be installed in the Canadian Patrol Frigates (CPFs), the TRUMPed *Tribals* and the *Annapolis* class ships.

Fraser also trialled the URN-20A Tactical Aircraft Beacon (TACAN), which gave the ship a unique appearance, as the TACAN was fitted on a prominent lattice mast between the funnels. In 1988 *Fraser* was the first Canadian ship equipped to operate with the HELTAS helicopter (a helicopter outfitted for a passive acoustic role). Trials of this system continued until the helicopter was lost in 1989.

On 18 October, 1993, she was one of three Canadian warships detailed to enforce United Nations sanctions off Haiti in OPERATION FORWARD ACTION. She returned to Halifax for the Christmas season, departing again on 8 January, 1994 for Haitian waters. On 10 January she suffered a minor boiler room fire which

FRASER on 19 November, 1967, as modified to a DDE.

injured four crewmen, though none seriously, and she was able to proceed to her patrol area. Relieved by *Annapolis* on 25 March, she arrived back in Halifax on the 30th. During the latter part of July, 1994, *Fraser* assisted the Dept of Fisheries in the seizure of the American fishing vessels *Warrior* and *Alpha Omega II*, reported to be illegally dragging for scallops on the Grand Banks. On 13-14 September, while on a FISHPAT, she towed the broken-down sailing vessel *Maja Romm* toward Canso, N.S., passing the tow to the *CCGS Simon Fraser* before returning to patrol.

After sailing more than 900,000 miles, *Fraser* made her final sail-past in Halifax on 5 October, 1994, and was decommissioned. This ceremony closed a chapter in Canadian history, *Fraser* having been the last of the *St. Laurent* class destroyers in commission.

FRASER, her appearance not too agreeably altered by the fitting in 1987 of a massive TACAN mast between her stacks.

She now replaces *Assiniboine* as a floating classroom at Halifax. The Canadian Naval Heritage Foundation has expressed an interest in making her into a museum. By May 1995, DND had agreed to postpone disposal of *Fraser* for a year with the hope that sufficient funds might be found to move the ship to Kingston, Ontario.

Battle Honours: Atlantic.. 1939-1940

The Heritage: *The first* Fraser *was a destroyer, the former HMS* Crescent, *which served in the RCN 1937-1940. She was sunk in collision with HMS* Calcutta *during the evacuation of France, 25 June, 1940.*

MARGAREE in the Fraser River near Ocean Falls, B.C., in 1958.

MARGAREE leaving Halifax on 10 September, 1969. The changes effected by conversion to a DDH, and the fitting of VDS, show clearly.

Margaree (2nd)

HMCS *Margaree* was built by Halifax Shipyards Ltd., and commissioned there on 5 October, 1957. She left Halifax on 1 November, and after refuelling stops in Havana, Balboa and San Diego, arrived in Esquimalt on the 27th to join the Second Canadian Escort Squadron.

On 16 January, 1958, the squadron departed Esquimalt for a major deployment. Convoy and anti-submarine exercises were carried out between port visits to Long Beach, Pearl Harbor, Yokosuka, Tokyo, Hong Kong, Saigon and Okinawa before the ships arrived back home on 2 April.

By her second birthday, *Margaree* had steamed some 70,309 miles and made 22 port visits.

During 1962, *Margaree* took part in JETEX '62 in the Pacific, along with *Assiniboine* and *Ottawa*. During these exercises, the Canadians worked with units from Britain, Australia, New Zealand, Fiji and India.

On 25 September, 1964, she began her conversion to DDH configuration at Victoria Machinery Depot, Victoria. Recommissioned on 15 October, 1965, she was retransferred for service on the Atlantic coast. In September 1976 she was one of

25

MARGAREE on 23 October, 1979, showing the pole mast fitted for TACAN between her stacks.

On 5 May, 1980, *Margaree's* DELEX refit was begun at Canadian Vickers Ltd., Montreal, but when it seemed likely that she would be ice-bound there, she was towed to Halifax and turned over on 10 December to SRU(A), where the work was completed in the summer of the following year. In succeeding years, she was several times Canada's representative in SNFA.

On 10 January, 1983, after 25 years of service and a refit completed by ship's company and dockyard staff, *Margaree* was able to carry out a full-power trial without any problems.

On 12-13 August, 1991, *Margaree* represented Canada in an historical re-enactment of the signing of the Atlantic Charter, 50 years earlier. The ceremony took place off Argentia, Newfoundland, with USS *Valdez* representing the United States.

After serving her country for 35 years, *Margaree* was decommissioned on 2 May, 1992. During her commissions, she had visited some 30 countries.

She was eventually turned over to Crown Assets, and on 3 February, 1994, sold to the Global Shipping Co., a Tampa, Florida firm, for $193,393.00. On 13 March, 1994, she left Halifax for the last time, under tow by the Russian tug *Afanasiy Nikitin*, bound for India to be scrapped.

four Canadian participants in the major NATO exercise Teamwork '76.

In January 1973 she joined the Standing Naval Force Atlantic along with HMCS *Protecteur* for a five-month tour. This was the first time two Canadian ships were a part of this force.

Battle Honours: Atlantic.. 1940

The Heritage: *The first* Margaree *was a destroyer, the former HMS* Diana*, which joined the RCN in 1940. She was lost in collision with a merchant ship on 22 October, 1940.*

Ottawa (3rd)

✪

HMCS *Ottawa* was built by Canadian Vickers Limited, Montreal. The third of the seven-ship *St. Laurent* class, she was commissioned on 10 November, 1956, and sailed for Halifax to join her sisters, *St. Laurent* and *Assiniboine,* in the Third Canadian Destroyer Squadron.

In June of 1957 she, along with *Assiniboine*, participated at an International Naval Review at Hampton Roads, Virginia.

In August 1957, an experimental deck was temporarily fitted over her stern to test the feasibility of landing a helicopter on a ship of this size. By the end of November *Ottawa* had crossed the Atlantic four times, engaged in two major NATO exercises and assisted HMCS *Bonaventure* in her work-up program off Northern Ireland. During the latter, further tests were carried out with the landing deck on *Ottawa's* quarterdeck.

In 1960, she was transferred to the west coast and the Second Canadian Escort Squadron. On 8 February *Ottawa,* along with *Saguenay* and *St. Laurent,* departed Esquimalt for a 2 1/2 month operational cruise across the Pacific. The ships carried out anti-submarine and tactical exercises as well as visiting Long Beach, Pearl Harbor, Yokosuka, Okinawa and Hong Kong. After a week's layover in Hong Kong

for self-maintenance, the ships departed 28 March, returning home via Okinawa, Kobe and the Aleutian Islands. The trio arrived back in Esquimalt on 29 April.

On 19-22 August of that year, *Ottawa* participated in the opening of the Pacific National Exhibition in Vancouver.

On 2 March 1961, *Ottawa*, with sister ships *Saguenay* and *St. Laurent*, departed Esquimalt for the Hawaiian Islands and three weeks of operations with the American Carrier Division 17 (USS *Kearsarge*). The ships returned home on 4 April.

OTTAWA in 1956.

27

OTTAWA as converted to a DDH 1963-64, and with the addition of a TACAN pole mast between her stacks.

In June 1963 she began her conversion to a DDH at Victoria Machinery Depot, Victoria. She was recommissioned on 28 October, 1964, the third of her class to complete this conversion, and left Esquimalt on 2 February, 1965 for service on the east coast, arriving in Halifax on the 26th.

In December 1968, she became the first naval unit to be designated a French Language Unit (FLU), with French used as the working language on board the ship.

In July 1976 she formed part of the escort to HMY *Britannia* during a Royal visit to Canada, and that September took part in a major NATO exercise, Teamwork '76. During this year she had logged 224 days away from home covering 40,151 miles, thereby making it one of her busiest years ever!

During 1977, *Ottawa*, along with *Margaree* and *Athabaskan*, visited the Soviet Union, following which she spent the last two months of the year with the SNFA, returning home in time for Christmas.

She returned to her builder, Canadian Vickers Ltd., for her DELEX refit between 19 April and 26 November, 1982.

After participating in the Navy's 75th Anniversary Naval Assembly in Bedford Basin in June of 1985, she headed for the Great Lakes. The purpose of this six-week cruise was to assist in recruiting, increase awareness of the Navy in central Canada and celebrate its 75th Anniversary. Nine port visits were made, and over 29,000 visitors toured the ship. One port visited was Midland, Ontario, (population 10,000) where some 7,000 people came aboard.

She was to serve again more than once with SNFA, and took part on 6-16 June, 1991, in the large NATO exercise Ocean Safari '91.

Ottawa was finally decommissioned on 31 July, 1992, in Halifax. During her service time, she had steamed over 600,000 nautical miles and visited ports in some 40 countries.

By February, 1994, she had been sold to Global Shipping of Tampa, Florida for $243,000, and on 4 April, 1994, left Halifax for the last time, under tow by the Russian tug *Sapfir*, bound for India to be broken up.

Battle Honours:		
	Atlantic	1939-1945
	Normandy	1944
	English Channel	1944
	Biscay	1944

The Heritage: *The first* Ottawa *was a destroyer, the former HMS* Crusader, *which joined the RCN in 1935. She was torpedoed and sunk in the North Atlantic on 13 September, 1942.*

The second Ottawa *was also a destroyer, the former HMS* Griffin, *which served the RCN 1943-1945. She was broken up in 1946.*

HMCS *Saguenay* (2nd)

✪

HMCS *Saguenay*, the fourth ship of the *St. Laurent* class, was built by Halifax Shipyards Limited, and commissioned in Halifax on 15 December, 1956.

During her first deployment, in 1957, she visited Chicoutimi, Quebec, where she was presented with the flag of the "Kingdom of Saguenay". So it was that she became the only Canadian warship permitted to fly a foreign flag, a tradition observed on 11 June of each year.

Saguenay served on the east coast as a member of the Third Canadian Destroyer Squadron until 1959, when she transferred to the west coast and the Second Squadron.

On 8 February, 1960, *Saguenay*, in company with *Ottawa* and *St. Laurent*, departed Esquimalt for a 2 1/2-month cruise across the Pacific. The ships carried out various exercises as well as visiting American and Japanese ports. After a week's layover in Hong Kong for self-maintenance, the ships departed on 28 March. Returning

SAGUENAY off the California coast, 5 December, 1959.

home via Okinawa, Kobe and the Aleutian Islands, the ships arrived on 29 April.

On 2 March, 1961, *Saguenay*, along with *Ottawa* and *St. Laurent*, departed Esquimalt for the Hawaiian Islands and three weeks of operations with the US Navy's Carrier Division 17 (USS *Kearsarge*). *Saguenay* distinguished herself with four "kills" in three days during these exercises. The ships returned home on 4 April.

On 22 August, 1963, she was paid off at Burrard Drydock Co. Ltd., North Vancouver, for conversion to a DDH, and recommissioned in this guise on 14 May, 1965.

Saguenay left Esquimalt that July to return to Atlantic Command, where she joined the First Canadian Destroyer Squadron.

On 15 July, 1970, she grounded at Port Hood, N.S., but was refloated the next day with no damage sustained.

In April 1971, she transferred to the Fifth Squadron. Her DELEX refit, started at Versatile Vickers, Montreal, on 29 October, 1979, was completed on 23 May, 1980.

On April 3, 1986, during a gunnery exercise off Osborne Head, near Halifax, a 3"/50 calibre shell misfired, injuring members of the gun crew and civilian technicians on board at the time. On 16 August, while on exercises in the Baltic Sea with the SNFA, *Saguenay* collided with the German *U 17*. Damage to both appeared upon inspection to be minor, and the ship continued with the exercise. At her next port of call, Haugesund, Norway, temporary repairs were made, but by 11 November a worsening vibration in the port shaft made further dockyard attention necessary. At Rosyth, Scotland, the propeller was removed and the ship made for Halifax, arriving on 5 December. Permanent repairs to the hull, shaft and propeller were completed and the ship returned to service by March 1987.

Saguenay's final deployment was a four-week tour of the Great Lakes in the summer of 1990. She was decommissioned on 26 June, in Halifax, where she languished alongside until purchased by the South Shore Marine Park Society, of Lunenburg, N.S. for

SAGUENAY after conversion to a DDH, and with TACAN pole mast added.

$1.00 in November, 1993. She was towed to Lunenburg on November 27, the Society's intention being to sink her between Cross Island and Sculpin Shoal, outside Lunenburg, as a "divers' wreck".

Saguenay made her final voyage on 25 June, 1994 when, shortly after 11 a.m., she was scuttled (taking 20 minutes and 11 seconds to slip below the waves) in 90 feet of water. She did not sink quite as planned, owing to a sand bar, and her mast was considered a hazard to navigation at low tide. However, by 11

May 1995, she had taken on a 70-degree list and was expected to settle even further on her starboard side.

Battle Honours:	Atlantic 1939-42

The Heritage: *The first* Saguenay *was a destroyer which served the RCN 1931-1945. She was broken up in 1946.*

SKEENA off the California coast, 21 November, 1960.

HMCS *Skeena (2nd)*

Built by Burrard Drydock & Shipbuilding, Ltd., at North Vancouver, *Skeena* was commissioned on 30 March, 1957. She was the third of the *St. Laurent* class to be built, and one of two built on the B.C. coast, the other being *Fraser.*

In 1957, during a visit to San Diego, her design (unusual for the time) gave rise locally to the rumour that she was nuclear-powered and capable of operating submerged! She almost put the rumour to the test when, in 1959, during a mid-Pacific storm, she survived a 57-degree roll.

On 16 January 1958, *Skeena*, along with other members of the Second Canadian Escort Squadron, left Esquimalt for eight weeks of exercises with US Navy units and a visit to several Far East ports. The squadron returned home on 2 April.

Skeena left Esquimalt on 26 May, 1964 for Halifax and, in July, began conversion to DDH configuration at Davie Shipbuilding Limited, Lauzon. Recommissioned on 14 August, 1965, she joined the Third Canadian Destroyer Squadron in Halifax, and in 1972 was designated the new French Language Unit for the fleet.

On 27 July, 1970, *Skeena* departed Halifax with *Protecteur* and *Annapolis* and headed for northern Canadian waters. The deployment was intended to provide experience operating and exercising in this area. Showing the flag to distant Canadian communities in connection with Manitoba's Centennial Year was also planned. Landfall was made at Fort Churchill, Rankin Inlet, Chesterfield Inlet and Wakeham Bay before the ships returned home in late September.

On 17 July 1976, *Skeena*, *Fraser* and *Protecteur* were in Montreal to provide a naval presence at the Olympics. Duties of the ships ranged from security and rescue crews at rowing events, emergency accommodation and support and the provision of security personnel as required. They headed back to Halifax on 4 August.

She underwent her DELEX refit at Montreal between 12 April and 20 November, 1981, arriving back in Halifax on the 30th of November, and commenced trials on 4 January, 1982.

SKEENA in 1974 after modification to a DDH, and with TACAN pole mast fitted.

On 21 May, 1985, *Skeena* was a member of Standing Naval Force Atlantic. The force was visiting Leixoes, Portugal, when a Soviet task group headed by the carrier *Kiev* passed Gibraltar during the night of 22-23 May. *Skeena*, along with USS *Richard F. Byrd*, left port and set a course to intercept the task group, which they did the following night. For the next two days the two western ships were interested observers of Soviet operations.

Skeena took part, 6-16 June, 1991, in the NATO exercise Ocean Safari '91, soon afterward visiting St. Lawrence and Great Lakes ports to encourage recruiting and public awareness. On August 31, 1991, she fired her 1,316th mortar round, the last to be fired by a Canadian warship.

After having sailed more than 980,000 nautical miles, she was decommissioned on 1 November, 1993. During her final sail-past in Halifax Harbour on that day, she treated herself to a 36-gun salute, one for each year of her service. On 3 July, 1996, she left Halifax in tow for India to be broken up.

Battle Honours:	Atlantic	1939-44
	Normandy	1944
	Biscay	1944

The Heritage: *The first* Skeena *was a destroyer which served in the RCN 1931-1944. She was wrecked near Reykjavik, Iceland, on 25 October, 1944.*

ST. LAURENT on December 12, 1963, showing the radical changes effected by her conversion to a DDH.

ST. LAURENT early in her career, about 1958.

HMCS *St. Laurent (2nd)*

★

The first ship of her class, *St. Laurent* was built by Canadian Vickers Ltd., Montreal, and commissioned on 29 October, 1955. She was unique of her class in that her main engines and turbines were built in Britain by Yarrows & Co. Ltd., Scotstoun, Glasgow, and shipped to Canada for installation.

St. Laurent made her maiden arrival in Halifax 5 November, 1955. On 17 February, 1956, she arrived at the U.S. Trials Center at Key West, Florida, to be extensively evaluated. The program involved not only *St. Laurent's* officers and crew but observers from Ottawa, as well as Trials Center personnel. She passed three months of tests with flying colours.

On 15 April, 1956, after negotiating the Potomac River at night, she arrived in Washington, D.C. at 0800 to show off Canada's newest warship to interested Americans, and on 5 May departed Halifax for the British Isles, again to "strut her stuff" for Admiralty officials. The latter seem to have been surprised that Canada was capable of producing so fine a vessel, and it was widely conceded that *St. Laurent* was the finest warship of her kind thus far built.

During this excursion, in June, she formed part of the escort to HMY *Britannia* on a state visit to Sweden. On board the *Britannia* at the time were the Queen, Prince Philip and the Earl of Mountbatten. Upon returning to the British Isles, *St. Laurent* visited the Port of London. Admiral Timbrell recalls that while secured there the ship received an unexpected visit from the Lords of the Admiralty. Timbrell, quickly recovering from his surprise, arranged a complete tour of the ship. One Sea Lord was overheard to inquire, "Why couldn't the RN come up with a ship like this?"

On 8 February, 1960, *St. Laurent*, along with two sisters, departed Esquimalt for a 2 1/2-month operational cruise across the Pacific. The ships carried out anti-submarine and tactical exercises, as well as visiting Long Beach, Pearl Harbor, Yokosuka, Okinawa and Hong Kong. After a week's layover in Hong Kong for self-maintenance, the ships departed on 28 March. They returned home on 29 April, with stops en route in Okinawa, Kobe and the Aleutian Islands.

On 2 March, 1961, she, along with *Ottawa* and *Saguenay*, departed Esquimalt to conduct exercises with the American Carrier Division 17 off Hawaii. The ships returned home on 4 April.

St. Laurent was test-fitted with a VDS system prior to being taken out of service for DDH conversion. Recommissioning in her new configuration took place on 4 October, 1963.

During the summer of 1969 she intercepted and tracked a Cuban-bound Soviet task force through Canadian waters.

She was paid off on 14 June, 1974, but remained in Halifax as a source of spare parts for her sister ships. In October 1979, she was sold to a local scrap dealer for $76,250. After stripping her of valuable metals the dealer resold her to a U.S. scrapyard for a reported $87,000. On New Year's Day, 1980, she left Halifax under tow by the tug *Odin Salvator* for Brownsville, Texas, to be broken up. On 12 January, however, she foundered in a gale off Cape Hatteras.

Battle Honours: Atlantic.. 1939-1945
Normandy.. 1944

The Heritage: *The first* St. Laurent *was a destroyer, the former HMS* Cygnet. *She served in the RCN 1937-1945, and was broken up in 1947.*

RESTIGOUCHE CLASS

This class was a natural follow-up to the *St. Laurent* class, with certain improvements, notably a 3"/70 calibre gun forward and a central fire control (Mk.69 director). When first installed, these guns had some teething problems. The Naval Armament Depot in Dartmouth withdrew the guns in their entirety (mount and mechanism down through three decks) and disassembled them. Some minor problems in the original installations were corrected, and the guns subsequently functioned perfectly.

This class was easily recognizable with the new gun mount, a higher bridge to give a better view over the gun, wing platforms attached to the foremast, and lookout wings just abaft the bridge.

By 1974 three of the class had been placed in reserve, eventually becoming stationary training ships until discarded.

Statistical Data					
Name	Pendant	Laid Down	Launched	Commissioned	Paid Off
CHAUDIÈRE	235	30/7/53	13/11/57	14/11/59	23/5/74
COLUMBIA	260	11/6/53	1/11/56	7/11/59	18/2/74
GATINEAU	236	30/4/53	3/6/57	17/2/59	
KOOTENAY	258	21/8/52	15/6/54	7/3/59	/12/95
RESTIGOUCHE	257	15/7/53	22/11/54	7/6/58	31/8/94
ST. CROIX	256	15/10/54	17/11/56	4/10/58	15/11/74
TERRA NOVA	259	14/11/52	21/6/55	6/6/59	

Displacement: 2,366 tons standard, 2,800 tons full load
As IRE: 2,390 tons standard, 2,900 tons full load
Dimensions: 366' x 42' x 13'6"
As IRE: 371' x 42' x 14'1"
Speed: Cruising - 14 knots; Maximum - 28 knots
Endurance: 4,750 n/m at 14 knots
Machinery: Geared Turbines: 2 shafts, 2 propellers, SHP: 30,000
Boilers: 2 Babcock & Wilcox water tube
Crew: 12 officers/237 men
As IRE: 13 officers/201 men

Armament: 2-3"/70 calibre Mk.6 (one twin mount): 90 rounds per minute to 10.5 miles; 2-3"/50 calibre Mk.33 (one twin mount): 85° elevation, 50 rounds per minute to 8 miles; 2 Mk.NC 10 Limbo, 3-barrelled, automatic-loading mortars, range - 3280 feet; Homing torpedoes.
As IRE: 2-3"/70 calibre Mk.6 (one twin mount: up to 90 rounds per minute to 10.5 miles; 1-Mk.112 ASROC launcher (with 8 reloads), range - up to 6 miles; 1-Mk.NC 10 Limbo 3-barrelled automatic-loading mortar, range - 3280 feet; 6-21 inch Mk.32 (2 triple) torpedo tubes, active/passive to 6.8 miles at 40 kts; 4 Super RBOC chaff launchers.

HMCS *Chaudière* (2nd)

✪

CHAUDIÈRE on 4 May, 1965. Her appearance was to remain essentially unchanged for the rest of her life.

HMCS *Chaudière* was built by Halifax Shipyards. In September 1958, during her fitting-out, a fire caused damage to the extent of $200,000. On 4 October two accidents occurred: one, a visiting engineer officer, died as a result of a fall, while another man barely missed being electrocuted. The last of the *Restigouche* class, the ship was commissioned on 14 November, 1959.

At the outset of her career, *Chaudière* operated out of Halifax as a unit of the Fifth Canadian Destroyer Squadron. She was subjected to a shock test during 1962 off Key West, Florida and, although basically undamaged, was out of service for 11 hours after the blast.

During February 1964, *Chaudière* took part in the NATO exercise Magic Lantern, off Gibraltar, and late that September left on a cruise to the U.K. She again departed Halifax on 4 May, 1965, on a cruise during which she made calls at Portland (U.K.), Copenhagen and Helsinki.

In October 1966, she located the missing boat *Puffin* in the North Atlantic. Sadly, the two crew members were not found, but the boat was returned to relatives of her owners.

On 2 October, 1967, *Chaudière* left Halifax to take up duties on the west coast. She was to be modernized (IRE conversion) at Esquimalt, but for reasons of economy the alteration was not carried out.

In 1970, it was announced that *Chaudière* would be one of three destroyer escorts whose complement would be reduced to that of training level during the year. She was decommissioned on 23 May, 1974 and subsequently cannibalized on behalf of other ships of her class. Her bow nose went in the summer of 1989 to replace that of *Kootenay* after the latter had been involved in a collision.

She was sold privately for $1.00 on 9 September, 1992, and sunk on 5 December in Sechelt Inlet, B.C., to become a "divers' wreck".

Battle Honours:	Atlantic	1944
	Normandy	1944
	Biscay	1944

The Heritage: *The first* Chaudière *was a destroyer, the former HMS* Hero, *which served in the RCN 1943-1945. She was broken up in 1950.*

COLUMBIA about 1959. Like *CHAUDIÈRE*, she never underwent IRE conversion.

HMCS *Columbia* (2nd)

The sixth of her class, HMCS *Columbia* was built by Burrard Drydock Co., Ltd, North Vancouver. She was commissioned on 7 November, 1959, and soon afterward left for service on the east coast.

On 9 September, 1960, *Columbia* sailed from Halifax to represent Canada at Nigerian independence celebrations. She returned to Halifax on 25 October after steaming 10,500 miles and visiting a number of African ports.

In March 1967, she departed Halifax in company with *Crescent* and *Algonquin* enroute to Esquimalt, for duty with Pacific Command.

Decommissioned on 18 February, 1974, *Columbia* served as a stationary training ship in Esquimalt, her propellers replaced with no-thrust "wheels", so that her engines might be run without leaving dockside.

Toward the end of June, 1996, she was sunk by the Artificial Reef Society of B.C., near Campbell River.

Battle Honours:	Belgian Coast	1914-1915
	Atlantic	1940-1944

The Heritage: *The first* Columbia *was a destroyer, the former USS* Haraden, *which joined the RCN in 1940. Irreparably damaged by grounding on 25 February, 1944, she was converted to an ammunition hulk and finally scrapped in 1945.*

HMCS *Gatineau* (2nd)

✪

HMCS *Gatineau* was built by Davie Shipbuilding, Lauzon, the first product of this company to join the postwar RCN. She was towed to Halifax by the tug *Foundation Vigilant* to avoid being icebound in the St. Lawrence River. The third of her class, she commissioned on 17 February, 1959, and began her service on the Atlantic coast.

In March 1968 *Gatineau* was the first Canadian warship to become a member of the newly formed Standing Naval Force Atlantic (SNFA). She took part in many Canadian, CANUS and NATO exercises.

She sailed from Halifax on 16 July, 1969, for Esquimalt, arriving there on 14 August. After being de-stored, she was turned over on 9 September to the SRU(P) facility to begin her $3.3 million *Improved Restigouche* class conversion.

GATINEAU on 15 September, 1959. Note the heightened bridge for vision over the larger gun mount, as compared with the **ST. LAURENTS**.

She was recommissioned on 14 April, 1971 and began sea trials (with her new mast 26 feet higher than the original, and stern modified to accommodate a VDS installation).

After successful completion of the trials, she joined the Second Canadian Destroyer Squadron at Esquimalt.

Departing Esquimalt on 28 August, 1972 in company with *Qu'Appelle* and *Provider*, the ship proceeded on a four-month South Pacific deployment. Exercises were conducted with units of Australia, New Zealand and the United States, and visits were made to ports in Hawaii, Tonga, Western Samoa, Fiji, Australia and New Zealand. 33,000 miles and three major exercises later, the ships returned home.

Gatineau began her DELEX refit in September 1981, the first west-coast ship to receive this treatment. She was recommissioned on 12 November, 1982.

On 15 April, 1987, she returned to Halifax, exchanging duties with *Huron*. During the fall of 1992, when operating with SNFA, *Gatineau* visited such widely scattered ports as Tallin, Estonia and Varna, Bulgaria.

She departed Halifax on 22 July, 1988 for a five-month tour with Standing Naval Force Atlantic. During this time she represented her country well for a 29-year-old ship, being one of only two ships (the other Dutch) to complete the tour without mechanical or other problems.

In July 1993, she played host to the cruiser *Marshal Ustinov* (along with two other Russian warships) during their visit to Halifax, the first such visit in 50 years. *Gatineau* escorted the departing visitors to international waters, carrying out exercises with them along the way—an odd circumstance after years of tension!

In the fall of 1993 *Gatineau*, along with *Fraser* and *Preserver*, represented Canada in the enforcement of UN sanctions off Haiti, *Gatineau* returning to Halifax on 23 November.

On 9 February, 1995, *Gatineau* departed Halifax to take part in the NATO exercise Strong Resolve off the coast of Norway from February 20 to March 10. For this exercise she was acting as flagship for the five-ship Canadian contingent. She returned to Halifax on 24 March. Ten April found her operating in support of Fisheries and Coast Guard ships off Newfoundland, enforcing Canada's position in the "Turbot Dispute" with Spain. From 19 to 30 June, as a member of Maritime Operations Group One, she participated in Exercise MARCOT 1/95 off the south coast of Nova Scotia.

For the rest of the year, *Gatineau* carried out workups and took part in Canadian fleet operations and fishery patrols. She was also present at the Miss Newfoundland pageant at Harbour Grace, Nfld. In February-March, 1996, she carried out two sovereignty patrols off the three Maritime provinces.

Her final sail-past was scheduled for 24 May, 1996 and as of 30 June she assumed an unmanned, extended readiness state, meaning that she could be made operational within 180 days.

GATINEAU on March 15, 1977, after IRE conversion. The towering mast is particularly prominent.

Her final decommissioning is expected in December 1998, as the Montreal Batch frigates come into service.

Battle Honours:	Atlantic	1943-1944
	Normandy	1944

The Heritage: *The first* Gatineau *was a destroyer, the former HMS* Express. *She served in the RCN 1943-1946, and was scuttled at Royston, B.C., as part of a breakwater in 1948.*

KOOTENAY departing Esquimalt on 21 June, 1994, to take part in UN operations off Haiti. As with ***GATINEAU***, her IRE modification is obvious.

KOOTENAY on November 4, 1964

HMCS *Kootenay* (2nd)

First of her class to be launched, *Kootenay* was built by Burrard's in Vancouver and commissioned on 7 March, 1959. After workups, she was transferred to the east coast. In November 1963, with *Columbia*, she was on hand at the Canadian Trade Fair at Philadelphia, and during February 1964 took part in the NATO exercise Magic Lantern off Gibraltar. In mid-August 1967, she visited Sault Ste. Marie during Centennial observances.

On 23 October, 1969, while on an overseas cruise, *Kootenay* suffered an explosion in her starboard gearbox which killed seven members of her crew and injured 53 others. She was towed first to Plymouth (part of the way by *Saguenay*), then by the tug *Elbe* to Halifax, where she arrived on 28 November. It had been the Navy's worst-ever peacetime accident.

While she was undergoing repairs, it was decided to convert her to IRE configuration. She was recommissioned in this guise on 7 January, 1972, and declared fully operational that September.

Kootenay left Halifax on 23 January, 1973 for Esquimalt, arriving there on 12 February. That May she was despatched to the South Pacific to provide standby support for Canadian Forces members serving in the International Commission of Control and Supervision (ICCS) in South Vietnam. On Canada's withdrawal from the ICCS on 31 July, she returned to Esquimalt, arriving on 16 August.

In July 1978, *Kootenay* assisted the RCMP in the seizure of $28 million worth of marijuana off the coast of British Columbia.

She started her DELEX refit on 25 October, 1982, at Halifax Shipyards, returning to service on 21 October, 1983.

On 8 May, 1986, along with *Provider*, *Restigouche* and *Terra Nova*, *Kootenay* departed Esquimalt to participate in the international exercise RIMPAC 86. The ships returned home on 21 June.

On 1 June, 1989, while exercising in thick fog without radar or navigating lights, *Kootenay* was involved in a collision with the M.V. *Nord Pol* approximately 28 miles off Cape Flattery, sustaining a three-foot by 16-foot gash in her bow above the waterline. The bow nose had been replaced with that of *Chaudière* in Esquimalt by 9 June, 1989. A court of enquiry later absolved her captain of any blame.

From 3 to 7 June, 1990, *Kootenay* visited Vladivostok, Russia, as part of a Canadian Task Group. (Other ships were *Annapolis* and *Huron*). They were the first foreign warships to enter the port since before World War 2.

Kootenay departed Esquimalt on 16 May, 1994, to participate in the semi-annual RIMPAC exercises in the Pacific. Then on 21 June, she left Hawaiian waters and proceeded to take part in OPERATION FORWARD ACTION (UN sanctions against Haiti), relieving *Terra Nova* on 13 July. Quitting Haitian waters on 15 September, she returned to Esquimalt. During the fall of 1994, she spent two weeks in a "showing the flag" and "coastal watch" tour of Canadian waters. The coastal watch program is organized by the RCMP to encourage citizens to report suspicious ships or happenings at sea. During this period she circumnavigated Vancouver Island.

Between January and early March 1995, *Kootenay* conducted three sovereignty patrols in southern B.C. coastal waters.

Her last operational mission saw *Kootenay* leave Esquimalt on 18 August, 1995, for South American waters. Along with *Athabaskan* from the east coast, she was to take part in a South American exercise which had been held annually for the past 36 years, but had never previously involved the participation of Canadian ships.

After exercising with the Chilean navy, *Kootenay* rounded Cape Horn on 16 October, an *ad hoc* sail being rigged so that it might be said that she had "sailed round the Horn". After further exercises with ships from Argentina, Brazil, Chile, the United States and Uruguay, she sailed back around the Horn for home. In memory of the four Canadian midshipmen who died at the Battle of Coronel 71 years earlier, a wreath was laid as the ship passed over the position where their ship, HMS *Good Hope*, was sunk.

After sailing nearly a million miles during her 36-year career, *Kootenay* was decommissioned on 18 December, 1995, to be stripped of reusable equipment and turned over to Public Works for disposal.

During the second week of January, 1996, the British Columbia Supreme Court handed down a decision on the collision of 1989. In a suit for damages, the court ruled that *Kootenay* was 70% at fault, and awarded the shipowners (Nordholm I-S of Copenhagen) $112,000.

Battle Honours:	Atlantic	1943-1945
	Normandy	1944
	English Channel	1944
	Biscay	1944

The Heritage: *The first* Kootenay *was a destroyer, the former HMS Decoy. She served in the RCN 1943-1945, and was broken up in 1946.*

RESTIGOUCHE entering Hong Kong on a Far East cruise. She graphically exemplifies the changed appearance brought about by IRE conversion.

HMCS *Restigouche (2nd)*

Restigouche was involved in a collision with the freighter *Manchester Port* on 27 November, 1957, in the St.Lawrence River, while still in the hands of her builder, Canadian Vickers Ltd.

She suffered damage to the port-side superstructure and hull, and was finally commissioned on 7 June, 1958 at Montreal.

That fall she visited Bermuda and Havana in the course of CANUS exercises. During an exercise with a U.S. submarine she actually landed two practice bombs on the hull of her submerged target!

She was present at the formal opening of the Seaway in June 1959, and at a NATO mini-review at Toronto the following month, immediately afterward carrying the Lieutenant Governor of Newfoundland on a tour of some of the province's outports.

Along with *Columbia*, she visited Washington, D.C., arriving there on April 29, 1961. The highly successful visit was followed with a call at Newport, R.I., the vessels returning to Halifax late in May. The purpose of this visit was to "show off" the new *Restigouche* class destroyers to interested American officials.

She sailed with the NATO "Matchmaker" squadron, forerunner of Standing Naval Force Atlantic, and took part in Exercise Magic Lantern off Gibraltar in February 1964.

Restigouche underwent her IRE modernization in 1970-72 at Halifax Shipyards, and in 1973 was transferred to the west coast, arriving in Esquimalt on 2 August. She commenced her DELEX refit there on 3 December, 1984, completing the process on 29 November, 1985.

RESTIGOUCHE on 11 April, 1964. Her gun mount is turned backward to lessen damage from seas.

On 11 March, 1991, *Restigouche* joined SNFA, the first Pacific-based ship to do so. On 24 February, 1992, she sailed via the Panama Canal to the Red Sea, for a six-month assignment with the multinational force convened to ensure that Iraq did not recommence hostile operations. For this operation she was armed as *Terra Nova* had been for her "Persian Excursion". She returned to Esquimalt via the Pacific on 18 August.

Decommissioned on 31 August, 1994, at Esquimalt, she awaits disposal.

Battle Honours:	Atlantic	1939-1945
	North Sea	1940
	Mediterranean	1943
	Normandy	1944
	Biscay	1944

The Heritage: *The first* Restigouche *was a destroyer, the former HMS* Comet. *She served in the RCN 1938-1945, and was broken up in 1946.*

ST. CROIX in 1962. Her appearance remained essentially unchanged throughout her career.

HMCS *St. Croix (2nd)*

✪

Second of the *Restigouche* class destroyers, *St. Croix* was built by Marine Industries Ltd., Sorel, and commissioned on 4 October, 1958 as a member of the Third Canadian Destroyer Squadron.

In 1959, as part of the Fifth Canadian Destroyer Squadron, she escorted HMY *Britannia* on a Royal visit to Canada, and in August 1960, with *Terra Nova*, helped mark the 500th anniversary of the death of Prince Henry the Navigator off Lisbon, Portugal.

In 1964 *St. Croix* transferred to the west coast, to remain there except for a few weeks' sojourn on the east coast early in 1966. On 4 May that year, she was subjected to an underwater shock test off San Francisco. She recovered her fighting efficiency after 30 minutes, a great improvement over *Chaudière's* test in 1962. The next day a second test, of increased severity, was conducted, and this time the ship was rendered "non-operational without dockyard assistance."

During 1967, and again in 1969, she visited Australia and New Zealand via Hawaii and Fiji.

Retransferred to the east coast in 1973, *St. Croix* served until 15 November, 1974, when she was paid off into Category "C" reserve. Her guns and propellers were removed, and her machinery spaces became classrooms for Canadian Forces Fleet School trainees until September 1990.

In 1991 she was purchased by Jacobson Metal of Chesapeake, Va., for $44,351.76, and towed out of Halifax in early April for scrapping.

Battle Honours:	Atlantic	1940-1943

The Heritage: *The first* St. Croix *was a destroyer, the former USS* McCook. *She joined the RCN in 1940 and was torpedoed and sunk south of Iceland on 20 September, 1943.*

TERRA NOVA in 1971. She demonstrates the top-heavy look imposed by the new mast installed during IRE conversion, and her ASROC launcher shows plainly at the after end of the superstructure.

TERRA NOVA on 10 March, 1959. Her after gun is unshielded, and she still flies the Red Ensign, being three months away from commissioning.

HMCS *Terra Nova*

Built by Victoria Machinery Depot, *Terra Nova* was commissioned on 6 June, 1959, the seventh and last of the *Restigouche* class, and shortly thereafter sailed for the east coast. She was present at the formal opening of the Seaway in July 1959, and at a review of NATO ships at Toronto in August.

In August 1960 she, along with *St. Croix*, was one of a number of ships from 15 countries assembled off Lisbon to commemorate the 500th anniversary of the death of Prince Henry the Navigator.

On 3 July, 1961, *Terra Nova* commenced a 12-day series of visits to Newfoundland outports, carrying the lieutenant governor of the province. The tour ended in Cornerbrook on 15 July.

In May 1965, *Terra Nova* entered Halifax Shipyards to commence the first part of her conversion to an *Improved Restigouche* class destroyer escort. She returned to service in February 1966, fitted with the new AN/SQS-505 sonar, which she tested for seven months. She then returned to the dockyard for completion of her conversion, returning to service in the fall of 1968. She had been the first of four of her class to undergo this process.

The Limbo mortar well of HMCS **TERRA NOVA**, about 1962. These ahead-throwing A/S weapons were loaded through ports in the side of the well, with the barrels in a horizontal position.

Terra Nova visited St. Pierre and Miquelon in 1967, along with *Skeena*, to escort to Montreal a number of French warships which were to take part in Expo 67 ceremonies.

During her first 12 years in service, *Terra Nova* participated in numerous national and multi-national exercises in the Atlantic, as well as in the North and Mediterranean Seas. She made visits to 35 different ports, including Oslo, Gibraltar, and Cartagena before reporting for duty on 4 May, 1971 at Esquimalt.

Terra Nova was part of the communications and standby support for Canada's contingent of the ICCS group off South Vietnam from 29 January to 8 June, 1973. She returned to Esquimalt on 26 June, 1973. In May 1983, she made a four-day visit to China on behalf of the Department of External Affairs and a Canadian trade fair.

She started her DELEX refit on 21 November, 1983 at Esquimalt, returning to service on 9 November, 1984.

In May 1986, she acted as escort to the Prince and Princess of Wales en route to Vancouver.

In June 1989, she returned to service following a nine-month refit which included the installation of a new torpedo decoy system (NIXIE) and the Canadian Electronic Warfare System (CANEWS).

On 12 December, 1989, she returned to the Atlantic Fleet, having exchanged bases and crews with *Annapolis*. Designated for service in the Persian Gulf conflict, she was temporarily armed with two quadruple Harpoon missile-launchers, mounted just behind the after deckhouse structure; a Phalanx gun mounted atop the Limbo well; 2-40mm single Bofors mounted amidships on the boat deck, and shoulder-fired Blowpipe and Javelin missiles. Accompanied by *Athabaskan* and *Preserver,* she left Halifax on 24 August 1990, not to return until 7 April, 1991.

During the summer of 1991 she carried out a five-week tour of the Great Lakes, visiting Oshawa, Hamilton, Midland, Goderich and Toronto before returning to Halifax on 24 August. The trip was organized to thank Canadians for their support during the Gulf conflict, as well as to show the ship and generate interest in the Navy.

By 5 February, 1992, *Terra Nova* had reverted to her original IRE configuration and resumed operations in her specialty field - ASW. That October she entered Port Weller Dry Dock, St. Catharines, Ontario, for a major refit, and a year elapsed before she was back in Halifax.

On 22 February, 1994, she stopped and boarded the M.V. *Pacifico* during a drug interdiction patrol, and escorted the ship into Halifax. The *Pacifico* proved to have been carrying 5.9 tonnes of cocaine, with an estimated street value of $1.2 billion.

Terra Nova relieved *Ville de Quèbec* on blockade duty off Haiti (OPERATION FORWARD ACTION) on 28 April, 1994. After spending some 87 days at sea, during which time she rescued two boatloads of refugees on two separate occasions, she arrived back in Halifax on 18 July. On 7 September she again headed for Haitian waters, arriving home on 19 October after the American occupation of Haiti.

On 10 March, 1995, *Terra Nova* was on a FISHPAT off Newfoundland when her age caught up with her. A small hole was found some six feet below the waterline near an air-conditioning pump. The hole was plugged and the ship remained on patrol until relieved by HMCS *Halifax* on 13 March. Returning to Halifax, she was drydocked for hull inspection and repairs which were completed at Halifax Shipyards on 30 March. Her hull was found to be in good condition. *Terra Nova* left Halifax on 20 April to attend the 50th Anniversary celebrations of VE-Day in Severmorsk, Russia, 7-10 May. En route there she made port visits in St. John's, Iceland and Norway. Upon departure from Russia, she headed for waters off Portugal to participate in the NATO exercise Linked Seas from 24 May to 6 June. Returning to Canadian waters, she called at St. John's and Sydney before joining Maritime Operations Group One for exercise MARCOT 1/95 off the southern coast of Nova Scotia. She returned to Halifax on 30 June.

On 16 July *Terra Nova* linked up at Quebec City with the Great Lakes portion of the visiting "Tall Ships", escorting the five sailing ships to Rimouski, Charlottetown and Louisbourg. There they joined with the Atlantic squadron of 15 Tall Ships and on 26 July re-enacted the siege of Louisbourg. *Terra Nova* was the official viewing stand for the event. She arrived back in Halifax on 31 July.

Terra Nova is expected to remain in service until July 1999. This would make her of one of the longest-serving ships in the Canadian Navy - some 40 years!

Battle Honours: Gulf and Kuwait.................................... 1991

MACKENZIE CLASS

Externally, this class differed little from the *Restigouche* class destroyers. Internally, they had a "communications control room" (CCR) replacing the message centre, radio one and radio three rooms. This CCR occupied the same space and included most of the equipment previously distributed in several compartments in the *Restigouche* and *St. Laurent* classes.

All four of these ships spent most of their operational lives on the west coast.

STATISTICAL DATA					
Name	Pendant	Laid Down	Launched	Commissioned	Paid Off
MACKENZIE	261	15/12/58	25/5/61	6/10/62	3/8/93
QU'APPELLE	264	14/1/60	2/5/62	14/9/63	31/7/92
SASKATCHEWAN	262	29/10/59	1/2/61	16/2/63	28/3/94
YUKON	263	25/10/59	27/7/61	25/5/63	3/12/93

Displacement: 2,380 tons standard, 2,880 tons full load
Dimensions: 366' x 42' x 13'6"
Speed: Cruising - 14 knots, Maximum - 28 knots
Endurance: 4,750 n/m at 14 knots
Machinery: Geared turbines, 2 shafts, 2 propellers, SHP: 30,000
Boilers: 2 Babcock & Wilcox water tube
Crew: 18 officers/210 men

As Training Ships: 10 officers/160 men + up to 40 officer cadets
Armament: 2-3"/70 calibre Mk.6 (one twin mount, forward): 90 rounds per minute to 10.5 miles; 2-3"/50 calibre Mk.33 (twin mount, aft): 85° elevation, 50 rounds/minute to 7.9 miles (*Qu'Appelle* had 2-3"/50 calibre forward); 2 Mk.NC 10 Limbo three-barrelled mortars, range 3280 feet; 6-21" Mk.32 torpedo tubes (two triple mounts) for Mk.46 torpedoes, active/passive homing to 6.8 miles at 40 knots.

HMCS *Mackenzie*

✪

The lead ship of the class, *Mackenzie* was built by Canadian Vickers Ltd., Montreal, and commissioned on 6 October, 1962. It is interesting to note that the only other *Mackenzie* in any of Her Majesty's navies was a Royal Navy trawler of World War 1.

Arriving in Halifax on 15 October, she spent the first five months of her service life operating from that port, perhaps as a result of the "Cuban Missile Crisis", but on 2 March, 1963, left for Esquimalt and never returned.

For the next 23 years she roamed the Pacific, either as a unit of the Fourth Canadian Destroyer Squadron or as part of Training Group Pacific. During the first three weeks of March 1964, she took part in the Commonwealth exercise JET 64, in the Indian Ocean, and on 22 February, 1965, left Esquimalt with *Saskatchewan* for a three-month cruise to the Far East.

On 4 May, 1970, *Mackenzie*, along with *Provider* and *Yukon*, headed across the Pacific once more. Exercises were carried out with units of the Australian, New Zealand, Japanese and American navies (with appropriate port visits) before the ships headed home.

A career highlight occurred on 30 June, 1973, when *Mackenzie's* crew boarded and seized the M/V *Marysville*, resulting in a million dollar "drug bust".

On 25 May, 1986, she began her DELEX refit, returning to service on 16 January, 1987. On 28 April, 1988, *Mackenzie*, accompanied by *Yukon* and four other Canadian ships, departed for a Pacific Rim tour, during which they exercised with units of the Japanese, Korean and American navies. After making a landfall in Hawaii on 21 June, the two ships headed for home.

Between 24 April and 30 June the following year she, along with other Canadian units, participated in SAMPLOY '89, the exercises being carried out between port visits in the United States, Mexico, Ecuador and Costa Rica.

After 30 years of service, during which she visited 96 foreign ports and sailed 845,640 nautical miles, she was decommissioned on 3 August, 1993.

In early March 1995, it was announced that *Mackenzie* would be sold to the Artificial Reef Society of B.C. The society made the ship environmentally safe, then scuttled her near Rum Island off Sidney, B.C. on 16 September.

Prior to this, she had been used as a set for a TV program. Painted in USN colours, she was the centrepiece of an episode of the program "X-Files" which was shown nationally on 10 March.

MACKENZIE on 25 July, 1964, off the California coast.

HMCS *Qu'Appelle (2nd)*

✪

Built by the Davie Shipbuilding Co., Lauzon, *Qu'Appelle* was commissioned on 14 September, 1963. As there was no 3"/70 calibre gun available when she was being constructed, a 3"/50 calibre gun was fitted forward. She was the fourth and final member of the *Mackenzie* class to be commissioned.

Qu'Appelle joined Pacific Command in the spring of 1964 and became a member of the Second Canadian Escort Squadron. At the end of August, 1971, in company with HMCS *Provider*, she conducted surveillance operations on a three-ship squadron of Soviet ships while they cruised from the Aleutians to the vicinity of Hawaii. This operation lasted for approximately two weeks.

On 28 August 1972, *Qu'Appelle*, in company with *Provider* and *Gatineau*, departed Esquimalt for a four-month South Pacific deployment. During this period exercises were conducted with units of the Australian, New Zealand and United States navies. Port visits included Hawaii, Tonga, Western Samoa, Fiji, Australia and New Zealand. 33,000 miles and three major exercises later, the ships returned home.

Qu'Appelle underwent her DELEX refit between 25 May, 1983 and 13 January, 1984. She sailed to Australia in the summer of 1986, with *Yukon* and *Saskatchewan*, to help celebrate the 75th birthday of the Royal Australian Navy.

For the last part of her operational service she was a member of Training Group Pacific, instructing junior officers.

Qu'Appelle was decommissioned on 31 July, 1992.

QU'APPELLE on 17 April, 1964, off the coast of California.

Battle Honours:	Atlantic	1944
	Normandy	1944
	Biscay	1944

The Heritage: *The first* Qu'Appelle *was a destroyer, the former HMS* Foxhound. *She served in the RCN 1944-1946, and was sold for breaking up in 1947.*

HMCS *Saskatchewan* (2nd)

*S*askatchewan was launched by the Victoria Machinery Depot Company (hull and superstructure), and completed by Yarrows Ltd. Esquimalt. She was commissioned on 16 February, 1963, at Esquimalt, the second of the *Mackenzie* class to enter service.

She transited the Panama Canal on 30 April, 1963, en route to Halifax, where she arrived on 3 June, but left again for the west coast on 20 October, arriving at Esquimalt on 29 November. It had been a busy year for *Saskatchewan*, with two transits of the Panama Canal, four Atlantic crossings and participation in a major NATO exercise.

Late in 1965, she was fitted with an eight-foot square bridge (made of aluminum and glass) atop her regular bridge, as part of an investigation into improved ways of conning a ship.

In February 1970, she returned to Atlantic Command with the crew of *Kootenay*, relieving *Nipigon* as flagship of SNFA. Mike Young, her X.O. during this period, recalls a social gaffe when the prewetting system was inadvertently turned on during a quarterdeck cocktail party in St. John's!

Saskatchewan returned to the west coast in 1973. She commenced her DELEX refit on 27 May, 1985, and returned to service on 17 June, 1986. That August she was part of a Canadian squadron which visited Australia for the RAN's 75th birthday celebrations.

In her final years, *Saskatchewan* was a member of Training Group Pacific, instructing as many as 40 officer cadets at a time in the finer points of ship-handling, navigation, and marine and combat systems engineering.

The ship completed a minor refit in 1990 which included the installation of an environmentally safe black-water system designed to reduce ship-generated pollution.

She was decommissioned on 28 March, 1994.

An excellent overhead view of **SASKATCHEWAN**, about 1961.

SASKATCHEWAN, probably 1968-69. Her appearance never appreciably changed during her service life.

Battle Honours:	Atlantic	1943-44
	Normandy	1944
	Biscay	1944

The Heritage: *The first* Saskatchewan *was a destroyer, the former* HMS Fortune. *She served the RCN from 1943 to 1946, when she was sold for breaking up.*

HMCS *Yukon*

✪

Built by Burrard Drydock Co., Ltd., North Vancouver, *Yukon* was commissioned on 25 May, 1963. She was the third of her class and the first ship of that name to join the RCN.

On 27 July, she sailed for Halifax, which was to be her home for the next 17 months. On 5 January, 1965, she sailed for Esquimalt, arriving there on the 26th to exchange crews with *Ottawa*, who had been ordered to Halifax.

On 4 May, 1970, *Yukon*, in company with *Mackenzie* and *Provider*, departed Esquimalt and headed west. The two destroyers arrived in Hakodate on 22 May, while *Provider* went to Yokosuka. During the voyage the ships carried out exercises with units of the Australian, New Zealand, Japanese and American navies. Between exercises the ships visited Kobe, Osaka and Sasebo before heading for home.

YUKON. Like **SASKATCHEWAN**, her appearance remained unchanged.

In February 1975 *Yukon* started her mid-life refit, following which she became a member of Training Group Pacific, taking on the role of instructing MARS officers.

She began her DELEX refit on 28 May, 1984, returning to the fleet on 16 January, 1985. In 1986 she was one of three RCN ships to visit Australia and take part in the RAN's celebration of its 75th birthday.

During her service life, *Yukon* steamed 792,181 nautical miles and visited ports in some 30 countries.

She was paid off on 3 December, 1993.

ANNAPOLIS CLASS

These two ships were the logical development of the *St. Laurent* through *Restigouche* and *Mackenzie* designs (although the 3"/50 mount was installed instead of the 3"/70). They were the first Canadian ships designed from the keel up as helicopter-carrying ships. Each cost approximately $31 million to build.

Statistical Data					
Name	Pendant	Laid Down	Launched	Commissioned	Paid Off
ANNAPOLIS	265	2/9/61	27/4/63	19/12/64	
NIPIGON	266	5/8/60	10/12/61	30/5/64	

Displacement: 2,400 tons standard, 2,930 tons full load
Dimensions: 371' x 42' x 14'4"
Speed: Cruising - 14 knots
Maximum - 28 knots
Endurance: 4,570 n/m at 14 knots
Machinery: Geared turbines, 2 shafts, 2 propellers
SHP: 30,000
Boilers: 2 Babcock & Wilcox water tube
Crew: 18 officers/210 crew

Armament: 2-3"/50 calibre Mk.33 (one twin mount): 85° elevation, 50 rounds/minute to 7.9 miles; 1 Mk.NC 10 Limbo three-barrelled, automatic-loading mortar, range - 3280 feet; 6-21" Mk.32 torpedo tubes (two triple); Mk.46 ASW active/passive homing torpedoes to 6.8 miles at 40 knots; 1 Sea King Helicopter

HMCS *Annapolis (2nd)*

Built at Halifax Shipyards Ltd., *Annapolis* was commissioned on 19 December, 1964 in Halifax, the 20th and final ship of the first postwar construction program.

On 27 July, 1970, *Annapolis*, along with *Protecteur* and *Skeena*, headed for northern Canadian waters in order to gain experience in high-latitude operation. Showing the flag at distant Canadian communities in connection with Manitoba's Centennial Year was a feature of the trip, and ports visited included Churchill, Rankin Inlet, Chesterfield Inlet and Wakeham Bay. The ships returned home in late September.

In June 1974, while serving as flagship of SNFA, *Annapolis* was responsible for saving a Canadian Sea King helicopter. The chopper was about to land on the American destroyer *Julius A. Furer* when it lost engine power. After rescuing its crew, *Annapolis* set about recovering the helicopter, which was kept afloat by flotation bags. The helicopter was towed to Den Helder, Holland, on a barge, then loaded aboard *Annapolis* and taken to Shearwater naval air station for repairs.

Annapolis underwent a major overhaul, 1978-79. Her DELEX/265 refit was begun on 19 August, 1985 at Saint John Shipbuilding Limited. It was expected to take 13 months, but changes in the process (based on experience with *Nipigon's* refit) extended it to 8 January, 1987.

ANNAPOLIS on 11 October, 1964.

A fine study of the VDS handling gear in **ANNAPOLIS,** 1970.

During this refit the VDS sonar and handling gear, as well as the mortar, were removed and replaced with a Canadian Towed Array Sonar System (CANTASS). The Nixie torpedo decoy system was also installed. A new gunnery control director was fitted, along with Super RBOC chaff launchers, two in the area of the former Limbo well and two on the bridge superstructure. A new lattice mast (similar to that of the *Improved Restigouche* class), with associated radars, was also installed.

The ship was also fitted with "Masker", a system consisting of two underwater belts - one before the boiler room and the other before the engine room. These release blankets of compressed air bubbles under the two compartments, trapping the noise between the belt and the hull, reducing the machinery sounds being transmitted into the sea. Cost of this refit came to more than $19 million - more than half of what it cost to build her.

Annapolis participated in a major NATO exercise (Ocean Safari '87) in the summer of 1987, and from 27 September to 3 October served as escort to the Royal Yacht *Britannia* on a tour of the Great Lakes. In mid-March, 1988, she began trials of the CANTASS system, to determine its suitability for the new patrol frigates currently being built.

On 14 August, 1989, she left Halifax for Esquimalt. With her arrival on 25 September, she became the first towed array-equipped vessel stationed on the west coast. From 3 to 7 June, 1990, *Annapolis* visited Vladivostok, Russia, as part of a Canadian Task Group which also included *Huron* and *Kootenay*.

On 25 March, 1994, she arrived off Haiti to participate in OPERATION FORWARD ACTION, during which, on 12 April, she suffered an explosion in her port boiler. There were no injuries, however, and the ship was able to continue her duties. *Annapolis* spent 30 days on this patrol before returning to Esquimalt after being relieved by *Ville de Quebèc*.

ANNAPOLIS at anchor in British waters, 18 July, 1980. A pole-mounted TACAN has been added.

In early 1995, *Annapolis,* as part of Maritime Operations Group Two, participated in an American Battle Group training exercise off Southern California.

Annapolis is expected to remain in service until just beyond the year 2000.

Battle Honours:	Atlantic..	1941-1944

The Heritage: *The first* Annapolis *was a destroyer, the former USS* Mackenzie. *She served in the RCN from 1940 to 1945, when she was sold for breaking up.*

ANNAPOLIS in 1993, flying off her Sea King. Note the IRE-style mast fitted during her DELEX refit, 1985-86.

HMCS *Nipigon* (2nd)

✪

The 35th ship built by Marine Industries Ltd., Sorel, for the RCN, *Nipigon* was commissioned on 30 May, 1964, and arrived in Halifax on 7 June, 1964.

On 18 October, 1965, while on exercises in the eastern Atlantic, tragedy struck *Nipigon*. A fire broke out in a fuel-handling room, killing one man and seriously burning others. Eight men were evacuated to the nearby HMCS *Bonaventure*.

Nipigon underwent her DELEX/265 refit between 27 June, 1983 and 22 August, 1984 at Davie Shipyard, Lauzon. Easily recognizable changes included the installation of the Improved *Restigouche*-type lattice mast, and a Mk.60 gunnery control system forward of it. Her draft was increased nearly a foot by the installation of almost 200 tons of ballast, to compensate for the removal of old equipment.

On 28 April, 1985, she provided SAR assistance to the fishing vessel *Lady Marjorie* off Halifax. The crew was rescued by the *Nipigon*, and as the fishing vessel was abandoned and on fire and therefore a hazard to navigation, it was decided to sink her by gunfire. This was done and the crew returned safely to shore. DND was later sued by the owner of the *Lady Marjorie* for sinking his vessel, when it could (in his opinion) have been salvaged. The case was eventually settled out of court, reportedly to the tune of nearly one million dollars.

In the spring of 1985, *Nipigon* was docked at Halifax Shipyard for repair of cracks in the plating near her forefoot. Further problems followed: on 1 June, she was turned over to SRU(A) after it was discovered that 210 rivets had been sheered off in the operations room from stress caused by the new mast installation. Repairs entailed the replacement of the rivets, further mast strengthening, 55 tonnes of additional ballast, the shifting of 40 tonnes of existing ballast, and replacement of a deck in "A" mess which had buckled. The total cost amounted to more than

$95,000. That fall, during exercises with SNFA, a bulkhead buckled behind the captain's cabin and several small holes appeared in the hull of the 25-year-old ship.

By April 1986, *Nipigon* had been fitted with CANTASS, and was conducting tests of the new system. The following month she had to return to drydock from exercises in the Caribbean, when a three-foot-long by three-foot-high crack appeared in her bow section below the waterline. Her structural problems seem to have ended once this was repaired.

On 27 February, 1987, her helicopter helped to rescue crewmen from the burning tug *Gulf Gale* off Cabo Rojo, Puerto Rico. That September the ship was designated as the second to have a mixed-gender crew (the first having been the diving support vessel *Cormorant*). This decision was implemented after a refit begun at Port Weller, Ontario on 30 August, 1988, and completed at Halifax on 16 February, 1990.

Now equipped with "separate gender facilities" for her ship's company, 25% of whom were women, she joined SNFA on 18 August, 1991.

On 16 May, 1993, *Nipigon* departed Halifax in company with HMNZ ships *Endeavour* and *Canterbury*, as Canada's representative at the 50th Anniversary of the Battle of the Atlantic ceremonies, held off the coast of Wales and at Liverpool.

In August 1993, she again began refit at Port Weller Drydock, and a year later was back in Halifax conducting post-refit maintenance.

One of five Canadian ships, *Nipigon* participated in the NATO exercise Strong Resolve off Norway from 20 February to 10 March 1995. She returned to Halifax on 24 March.

Nipigon left Halifax on 7 April to support Fisheries and Coast Guard ships off Newfoundland enforcing Canada's position in the "Turbot Dispute" with Spain. On 14 June crew members, along with a DFO enforcement officer, boarded the Spanish trawler *Patricia Nores* and found 11 tonnes of turbot over the amount recorded in the ship's log.

From 19 June to 30 June, as part of Maritime Operations Group One, she participated in MARCOT 1/95 in St. Margaret's Bay and along the south coast of Nova Scotia.

On 4 March, 1996, she was dispatched from Halifax to the aid of HMCS *Okanagan*, whose emergency beacon had been activated. Fortunately, it proved to have been released accidentally, and unknown to those in the submarine.

Nipigon is expected to remain in service until just beyond the year 2000.

Battle Honours:	Atlantic... 1941-1945

The Heritage: The first Nipigon *was a Bangor class minesweeper which served in the RCN 1941-1946. Transferred to the Turkish Navy in 1957, she served as* Bafra *until 1972.*

IROQUOIS CLASS					
Statistical Data					
Name	Pendant	Laid Down	Launched	Commissioned	Paid Off
ALGONQUIN	283	1/9/69	23/4/71	3/11/73	
ATHABASKAN	282	1/6/69	27/11/70	30/9/72	
HURON	281	6/69	9/4/71	16/12/72	
IROQUOIS	280	15/1/69	28/11/70	29/7/72	

Displacement: 3,551 tons standard, 4,200 tons full load
TRUMPed: 3,551 tons standard, 5,150 tons full load
Dimensions: 398' (425' oa) x 50' x 14'
Speed: Cruising - 18 knots
Maximum - 29+ knots
Endurance: 4,500 n/m at 20 knots
Machinery: COGOG (Gas turbines): 2-FT4A2 Pratt & Whitney gas turbines, 2 Pratt & Whitney FT12AH3 gas turbines; 2 GM Allison 570 KF gas turbines;2 shafts, 2 five-bladed, controllable-pitch propellers, SHP: 50,000
Crew: 14 officers/230 men
Armament: 1-5"/54 calibre OTO Melara dual-purpose (single mount) 45 rounds/minute to 9.3 miles; 1 Mk.NC 10 Limbo

3-barrelled, automatic-loading mortar, range 3280 feet; 6-21" Mk 32 torpedo tubes (2 triple mounts): active/passive to 6.8 miles at 40 knots; Two quadruple Sea Sparrow surface-to-air missile launchers (P & S), semi-active radar homing to 9 miles; 32 missiles carried; 1-4" illumination rocket launcher; 2 Corvus chaff rocket launchers; 2 Sea King helicopters

TRUMPed: 1-3" OTO Melara rapid fire gun; 1 Phalanx close-in gatling gun; Standard surface-to-air missiles, Mk. 41 vertical launch system: 29 missiles carried; 6-21 inch Mk.32 torpedo tubes (2 triple mounts): Chaff Plessey Shield Infrared Missile decoy system; 2 Sea King helicopters

NIPIGON on 7 June, 1964. Recently commissioned, she was the first DDH to be launched in that format.

ALGONQUIN showing the considerable changes effected by TRUMP modification, 1987-91. Most obvious, perhaps, is the combination of the original two stacks into one square casing. Notable, too, is the vertical launch system behind the foc'sle breakwater, and the new 3" gun on the platform in front of the bridge. A new, long-range fire control radar (AN/SPS-49) is sited forward of the mast.

HMCS *Algonquin* (2nd)

✪

Fourth of her class and built at Lauzon by the Davie Shipbuilding Co., *Algonquin* was commissioned on 3 November, 1973, to be based in Halifax.

In November 1974, she rescued seven crew members from the fishing vessel *Paul & Maria*, which was in distress 80 miles east of Halifax.

During Caribbean exercises in the winter of 1977, she visited Rio de Janeiro, Brazil, and thus became the first of the new *Tribals* to "cross the line".

On 26 September 1978, *Algonquin* relieved *Huron* as flagship of STANAVFORLANT in Plymouth, England. She stayed with the force until 31 December of that year.

By November 1983, she had steamed more than 200,000 miles, in the process actually spending a total of three years at sea. She had participated in more than 20 major multi-national exercises and completed four tours with SNFA, three of them as flagship.

On 1 March, 1986, *Algonquin* rendered assistance to the Department of Fisheries and Oceans. The Panamanian vessel *Peonia 7* had been boarded off the Grand Banks and ordered to proceed to St. John's, but its captain refused and headed out of the 200-mile EEZ with two Fisheries officers on board. The Fisheries vessel *Cape Rogers*, in pursuit, requested DND assistance, and she and *Algonquin* overtook the *Peonia 7* and escorted her into St. John's.

On 26 October, 1987, *Algonquin* commenced her scheduled 18-month TRUMP refit at MIL Davie, Lauzon. Four years later, after labour problems, contract disputes and specification changes, she was provisionally returned to the Navy on 11 October, 1991, although trials were to continue until the summer of 1992.

ALGONQUIN on 15 November, 1973, exhibiting her oddly-angled "rabbit-ear" funnels. The boxlike structure against the front of the bridge houses the Sea Sparrow launcher, and the spherical-topped fire control radars figure prominently ahead of the mast. All of these features disappeared in the course of her TRUMP refit.

Fifteen November, 1991 saw *Algonquin* alongside in Halifax, conducting inclination trials. In the course of these, she took on too much water and heeled to 25 degrees—5 more than the trials were designed for. After righting, it was discovered that three living spaces and part of the engine room had been flooded.

In March 1993, she was declared fully operational from her TRUMP refit, and on the 29th of the month left Halifax to join SNFA as flagship. On 24 June, 1993, *Algonquin* passed through the Strait of Otranto into the Adriatic Sea, to join other NATO and allied forces in enforcing a blockade of the former Yugoslavia. The blockade was intended to stop war supplies from reaching the various warring factions within the country.

Fifteen October, 1993, saw *Algonquin* return to Halifax after her six-month tour with SNFA. Four months had been spent in the Adriatic Sea with the UN force.

SRU(A), Litton Systems and MIL staff now set about replacing her computers, improving software, making structural repairs to her mast and fuel systems, and adding two new navigational radars. She was then drydocked to receive new propeller blades.

Following a series of sea trials and inspections, *Algonquin* was transferred to the west coast, arriving there in August 1994. She is one of three vessels in the fleet designated as a French-language unit.

In early 1995 *Algonquin*, as part of Maritime Operations Group Two, participated in an American Battle Group training exercise off Southern California. That fall she was the first west-coast ship to fire the Standard Mark 2 Block 2 surface-to-surface missile, which she did at the Pacific Missile Test Range in the Hawaiian Islands.

The following spring she participated in Exercise Westploy '96, acting as flagship of a group including *Protecteur*, *Regina* and *Winnipeg*. During the three-month exercise the ships visited Japan, the Soviet Union and South Korea, and afterward took part with Korean units in Rimpac '96, in Hawaiian waters.

Battle Honours:		
	Norway	1944
	Normandy	1944
	Arctic	1944-1945

The Heritage: *The first* Algonquin *was a destroyer, the former HMS* Valentine. *She served in the RCN 1944-1970, and was broken up in 1971.*

HMCS *Athabaskan (3rd)*

T he third of her class, *Athabaskan* was built by Davie Shipbuilding Co., Lauzon, and commissioned on 30 September, 1972.

On 26 November, 1981, while in company with *Algonquin* and *Preserver*, she was dispatched in response to an SOS from the 575-foot M/V *Euro Princess*, badly holed and drifting down onto the oil rig *Rowan Juneau*, off Sable Island. The crew of the ship were rescued by helicopters, while *Athabaskan's* Sea King removed 44 people from the rig itself, in 60-knot winds and sea state 5 conditions. Due to a failure of the recovery cable of the "Beartrap" system, landings on the *"Athabee"* had to be very skilfully done.

By 2 November, 1982, her tenth birthday, the ship had travelled some 267,000 miles. Late in 1988, she grounded in Norway's Vestfjord while attempting to assist the already grounded Belgian frigate *Westhinder*.

On 24 August, 1990, *Athabaskan* departed Halifax as one of three ships representing Canada in operations during the Persian Gulf conflict. She had been fitted for the purpose with a Phalanx gun system atop her Limbo well, and a single 40mm Bofors to port and starboard on her boat deck. As flagship of Canada's task group, she assisted in enforcing UN sanctions and participated in the liberation of Kuwait. She returned to Halifax on 7 April, 1991.

In October 1991, she was handed over to Marine Industries Limited, Lauzon, for her TRUMP refit. This completed, she returned to Halifax on 9 June, 1994, and was provisionally accepted on 3 August. *Athabaskan* was then scheduled to undergo some enhancements which had not been a part of the TRUMP refit. These included the installation of a Pathfinder radar, Nixie torpedo system, reverse osmosis distillers and the fitting of an interim black-water fit. After extensive post-refit trials, the ship was finally accepted by the Navy in May 1995.

ATHABASKAN in her original guise, providing a good view of her VDS and its handling gear, her Limbo well, flight deck and "two-helicopter garage".

On 22 June 1995, *Athabaskan* was off Roosevelt Roads, Puerto Rico, where she successfully tracked and engaged an inbound drone travelling at sub-sonic speed with one of her SM 2 Block 3 missiles.

On 8 October she headed for Uruguay for a two-month naval exercise called UNITAS. Ships from Argentina, Brazil, Chile, Spain, the United States and Uruguay participated. *Kootenay*, from the west coast, was the other Canadian participant. This was the first time in 17 years that Canadian navy ships had visited the South American continent and the first time they had ever taken part in this annual exercise. *Athabaskan* returned to Halifax on 5 December.

Battle Honours:		
	Arctic	1943-1944
	English Channel	1944
	Korea	1950-1953
	Gulf and Kuwait	1991

The Heritage: *The first* Athabaskan *was a destroyer which joined the RCN in 1943. She was torpedoed and sunk in the English Channel on 29 April, 1944.*

The second Athabaskan, *also a destroyer, served in the RCN 1948-1966. She was broken up in 1970.*

HMCS *Huron* (2nd)

✪

Second of the class, and built by Marine Industries Ltd, Sorel, *Huron* was commissioned on 16 December, 1972. She represented Canada at the Silver Jubilee naval review at Spithead, off Portsmouth, on June 28, 1977.

During her refit, September 1979 to April 1980, *Huron* had her C3 sonar dome fixed in the "down" position and fared into the hull. This was done to minimize turbulence noise caused by the edges of the dome in its retracted position.

In March 1980, while on patrol off Nova Scotia, she rescued 21 crew members from the freighter *Maurice Desgagnes,* whose hull had been punctured by her cargo of railway ties.

Huron took part in exercises in the Mediterranean during the last week of April 1980, her first time in those waters. She was utilized as a trials ship for the vertical-launched Sea Sparrow system the following year. The weapon was tested in Roosevelt Roads, P.R., 19-24 February, 1981.

Between 18 May and 3 June, 1981, she carried Governor-General Edward Schreyer on a tour of five Scandinavian ports.

On 17 July, 1987, *Huron* joined Pacific Command and the Second Canadian Destroyer Squadron, the first modern Tribal to serve on that coast. *Gatineau* was transferred in her place to the east coast. *Huron* quickly became an integral part of the Second Destroyer Squadron and a kingpin in the Canadian Task Group Pacific.

On 26 November 1989, *Huron* completed a $2 million refit in Port Weller Drydock, St. Catharines, Ontario. This was the first time in a number of years that a refit had taken place in a Great Lakes shipyard. During the refit new propellers were installed, the shafts and rudder re-sleeved, underwater hull fittings replaced, some stability tanks converted into fuel tanks, and some watertight doors fitted. Tanks and bilges were cleaned, and the ship completely repainted. She returned to Halifax on 14 December.

Between 3 and 7 June, 1990, she led a Canadian Task Force (*Kootenay* and *Annapolis* being the other two participants) in a visit to Vladivostok, Russia. This was the first Canadian military formation to enter that port since before World War 2.

On 24 February, 1991, she departed Halifax en route to relieve *Athabaskan* in the Persian Gulf, returning home to Esquimalt on 2 August. For this operation she was armed as the *Athabaskan* had been.

By July 1993, *Huron* was at Marine Industries Ltd., Lauzon, undergoing her TRUMP refit. The last of the class to undergo this refit, she returned to Halifax on 25 November, 1994, to begin naval and contractors' trials. Leaving Halifax on 21 June, 1995, she headed for the west coast, and after stops in Curaçao, Puerto Vallarta and San Diego, arrived in Esquimalt on 21 July, 1995.

Battle Honours:		
	Arctic	1943-1945
	English Channel	1944
	Normandy	1944
	Korea	1951-1953

The Heritage: *The first* Huron *was a destroyer which served in the RCN 1943-1963. She was broken up in 1965.*

HURON on 22 November, 1972

HMCS *Iroquois* (2nd)

★

First of the "280" class, she was built by Marine Industries Ltd., Sorel, and commissioned on 29 July, 1972.

Doc Macgillivray, the *Iroquois'* first captain, tells of experiencing a 55-degree roll. In late 1972 the ship paid a visit to Boston, Mass., for the benefit of various industrial concerns, and to show her off to U.S. Naval officials. During the second week of December, the ship was returning to Halifax when she found herself in an unexpected winter storm. A sudden shift of the wind abeam forced the ship over to the point where the inclinometer hit its side and stayed there. It was only after several anxious moments that she slowly righted herself!

During her first few years of service, *Iroquois* was used as a trials ship for her class, testing equipment or improvements to be used in or made to her class.

On 17 April, 1978, *Iroquois* left Halifax and began a typical NATO deployment. She took part in a major exercise off Portugal, operated with French units in the Bay of Biscay, then carried out exercises with German units off the coast of Denmark. Visits to the ship were made by NATO Headquarters staff off Portland, U.K. followed later by a brief visit from the Supreme Allied Commander Europe. Two close surveillance taskings of Soviet ships were sandwiched in between. *Iroquois* returned home on 7 July after steaming some 14,300 miles.

On December 4, 1983, while on a routine FISHPAT (Fishery Patrol) on the Grand Banks, *Iroquois* intercepted a request for assistance from the *Ho Ming 5*, a Panamanian-registered freighter which was in danger of capsizing due to a shifted cargo. In high seas and gale winds, 11 of the 20-man Korean crew were saved by the ship's Sea King, while 9 others were rescued by Zodiac inflatable boats. For their efforts, 12 crew members of the *Iroquois* were awarded the Star of Courage and six others the Medal of Bravery. During this operation the ship took on a similar roll (55 degrees) to the one which had taken place in late 1972. Of interest is the fact that *Iroquois* is the only vessel of her class to report such a roll, let alone two of them.

On 4 July 1986, *Iroquois*, along with ships from 25 other nations, attended an International Naval Review in New York. This review was a part of the celebration of the 100th Anniversary of the Statue of Liberty.

She started her TRUMP refit on 1 November, 1989, and was provisionally accepted back into the fleet on 3 July, 1992. Shortly afterward she sailed for Charleston, S.C., where she loaded her full complement of 29 vertically-launched Sea Sparrow missiles. *Iroquois* then departed for Roosevelt Roads, P.R., where later that month she conducted successful test firings of the missiles.

She departed Halifax on 25 September, 1993, to join the NATO fleet off the coast of the former Yugoslavia, enforcing UN sanctions against the warring factions of that area. She replaced *Algonquin* on that duty, returning to Halifax on 25 April, 1994 after being relieved by HMCS *Halifax*.

On 7 March 1995, *Iroquois* departed Halifax bound for the Caribbean. After picking up her full complement of the SM2 Block 3 anti-air missiles at Yorktown, Virginia, she again proceeded to the Roosevelt Roads test firing range. On 19 March she successfully launched a missile against a sea-skimming target. This was the first live firing of an SM2 by a Canadian ship. Then on 21 March she launched another SM2 at a target some 50 miles away. Again, another hit. Anti-submarine, boarding and chaff exercises followed before the ship arrived back home on 6 April.

On 17 June *Iroquois* took over as flagship for Maritime Operations Group One from *Terra Nova* in St. John's.

On 22 February, 1996, she departed Halifax as flagship of the six-ship East Coast Task Group, which after workups in the Caribbean, took part in the major NATO exercise Unified Spirit off the U.S. east coast. They returned to Halifax on 3 April.

Iroquois is one of three designated francophone units of the fleet.

IROQUOIS
on 15 August,
1972.

Battle Honours:	Atlantic	1943
	Arctic	1943-1945
	Biscay	1943-1944
	Norway	1945
	Korea	1952-1953

The Heritage: The first Iroquois *was a destroyer which served in the RCN 1942-1962. She was broken up in 1966.*

CANADIAN PATROL FRIGATES
CITY CLASS - *HALIFAX* BATCH

The twelve ships of this class are named after capital cities in Canada. The Canadian Navy traditionally assigns hull numbers in the 300 series to frigates, a practice which continues with these ships.

Statistical Data					
Name	Pendant	Laid Down	Float-up	Prov. Acc*	Paid Off
CALGARY	335	15/6/91	28/8/92	30/8/94	12/5/95
HALIFAX	330	19/3/87	30/4/88	28/6/91	29/6/92
REGINA	334	6/10/89	25/10/91	2/3/94	30/9/94
TORONTO	333	22/4/89	18/12/90	23/12/92	29/7/93
VANCOUVER	331	19/5/88	8/7/89	11/9/92	23/8/93
VILLE de QUÉBEC	332	16/12/88	16/5/91	23/9/93	14/7/94

* Indicates the ship became "navy" manned and operated, a prerequisite to the commencement of trials whose nature or complexity prohibits the contractor from performing them independently.

Displacement:	4,750 tonnes
Dimensions:	440' x 53'8" x 15'1"
Speed:	29+ knots (designed)
Endurance:	7,100 miles at 15 knots (diesel)
	4,700 miles at 15 knots (gas)
Machinery:	1 Pielstick Model PA6, 20 cylinder cruise diesel;
	2 GE LM2500 gas turbines; 2 shafts;
	2 controllable-pitch propellers
Crew:	185 (peace) - 225 (war)
Armament:	1 Bofors 57mm MK 2 rapid-fire gun: 75° elevation, 220 rounds/minute to 10.5 miles;

1 Phalanx close-in Gatling gun MK15: 3000 rounds/minute to .9 miles;
6 sites for heavy machine guns;
16 Sea Sparrow Surface-to-air missiles, semi-active radar homing to 8.7 miles;
8 Harpoon Surface-to-surface missiles (two quad launchers: infra-red homing to 80 miles;
4-21" MK46 (2 twin) homing torpedo tubes: active/passive to 6.8 miles;
SHIELD offboard infra-red and CHAFF decoy systems

CALGARY in 1994.

HMCS *Calgary* (2nd)

The final ship from MIL, *Calgary* was launched on 28 August, 1992 and, after fitting out, commenced builder's sea trials in the spring of 1994.

She departed Quebec City on 24 June, 1994, for Halifax, making her maiden arrival there on 28 June. She was provisionally accepted in a short ceremony held at Shearwater on 30 August, 1994.

After undergoing trials to ensure that she met contract specifications, she departed Halifax on 25 November, bound for Esquimalt. After stops in Aruba and San Diego, she arrived at her new home on 23 December.

Calgary was commissioned on 12 May, 1995 at Esquimalt.

On 10 July, 1995, *Calgary* proceeded on her first operational mission - a trip to the Arabian Gulf. On 11 August, after steaming some 12,000 miles, she arrived in the Gulf of Oman and joined the Multinational Interdiction Force (MIF) in enforcing UN sanctions against Iraq. From mid-October through November she was a member of NATO's Standing Naval Force Mediterranean in the Adriatic. This was the first time a Canadian ship had operated with this force.

On 2 December *Calgary* was returning home via the Atlantic when a request for assistance was received. The Greek bulk carrier *Mount Olympus* was 1500 kilometres south of Halifax and in danger of sinking. *Calgary* headed for the scene, some 900 kilometres away. When 80 kilometres from the bulk carrier, she launched her helicopter. The helo arrived on the scene and rescued all 30 people aboard during four trips, depositing them aboard the Bulgarian freighter *Rodopi*, which was standing by the stricken *Mount Olympus* but could not lower boats.

Calgary returned to Esquimalt on 22 December, having become the first CPF to circumnavigate the globe.

Battle Honours:		
	Atlantic	1942-1945
	Biscay	1943
	Normandy	1944
	English Channel	1944-1945
	North Sea	1945

The Heritage: *The first* Calgary *was a corvette which served in the RCN 1941-1945. She was broken up in 1951.*

HALIFAX

HMCS *Halifax* (2nd)

✪

The lead ship of the class, *Halifax* was commissioned at her namesake port on 29 June, 1992. She was the first new Canadian warship to be commissioned since *Algonquin (2nd)* on 3 November, 1973.

In August 1992, she departed Halifax for a tour of inland Canada to show Canadians the latest addition to their seagoing arsenal. Calling at ports from Charlottetown to Toronto, the ship received more than 30,000 visitors.

On 15 March, 1993, she assisted the USN in search efforts for a downed Tomcat aircraft off Norfolk, Virginia. With her state-of-the-art equipment, *Halifax* was able to pinpoint the exact location of the crash. Between the 27th and the 30th of the same month, while off Puerto Rico, she successfully tested her Harpoon and vertical-launched Sea Sparrow systems against "hostile" targets.

By the fall she had completed her first-of-class and combat trials, and became fully operational in a ceremony held at Halifax on 20 December, 1993. On 30 December, she reported for sea duty (i.e., on four-hour standby for such duties as search and rescue, drug interdiction and general patrolling).

On 2 April, 1994, she departed Halifax for a five-month deployment with the NATO fleet enforcing the UN embargo off the former Yugoslavia. She thus became the first of her class to participate in an operational mission. One day after departing Halifax, the ship suffered a malfunction with her diesel engine when it overheated and a computer shut it down. Tiny cracks had appeared in the connecting rods and the bolts which hold them in place. The manufacturer, S.E.M.T. Pielstick, sent technicians to meet the ship in the Azores, but they were unable to find the root of the problem. *Halifax* continued on, using her gas turbines only. Until the problem could be fixed, all ships of the City class had their speed restricted to 15 knots when using their diesels. *Halifax*

relieved *Iroquois* on 15 April. After an uneventful mission, she returned to base on 9 September.

On 28 October, while anchored in Bedford Basin, a leaking fuel line caused a small fire on board the ship. Damage control sensors shut off the fuel supply and the fire was extinguished immediately.

In mid-November 1994, *Halifax* was subjected to three shock tests some 330 kilometres off Nova Scotia. The final and largest explosion took place at 1205 on 18 November, when 10,000 pounds of HBX1 was set off 230 metres from the ship. She withstood the tests with no adverse effects other than some cracked pipes and a temporary radar malfunction.

On 5 December, 1994, *Halifax* entered drydock to effect repairs to her diesel engines as well as other work. New rods, crankshaft and the bottom part of the engine block were replaced (S.E.M.T. Pielstick assuming the cost) and the ship returned to service on 10 March, 1995. She left Halifax the next day to relieve *Terra Nova* on fisheries patrol off Newfoundland.

On 20 April she left Halifax once again, this time bound for Europe to take part in VE-Day celebrations. She visited Iceland, Norway and Poland. After leaving Gdynia, Poland on 15 May, *Halifax* proceeded to waters off Portugal to participate in the NATO exercise Linked Seas. She arrived back in home waters on 16 June, securing in Sydney, N.S. due to the G-7 Summit being held in Halifax. After a two-day visit, she joined Maritime Operations Group One and participated in exercise MARCOT 1/95 off the south coast of Nova Scotia. She returned to Halifax 30 June.

On 18 March, 1996, *Halifax* sailed for her second deployment in the Adriatic with STANAVFORLANT.

Battle Honours: Atlantic.. 1942-1945

The Heritage: *The first* Halifax *was a corvette which served in the RCN 1942-1945. She was sold in 1946.*

REGINA arriving at Esquimalt, 20 July, 1994

HMCS *Regina* (2nd)

✪

The second of the MIL-built ships, *Regina* was launched seven months earlier than planned, on 25 October, 1991. In order to keep her centre of gravity low, her mast, funnel and part of the superstructure had yet to be fitted when the ship was launched, which brought her launching weight down to approximately 3,000 tonnes.

Builder's sea trials began in August 1993, and she arrived in Halifax for the first time on 5 December. *Regina* was provisionally accepted by the Navy on 2 March, 1994, and carried out further trials until departing Halifax on 13 June for her new home, Esquimalt. She arrived there on 20 July, stopping en route at Charleston, Aruba and San Diego.

She is the second of the CPFs to operate from the west coast and the seventh to be commissioned, the latter ceremony taking place on 30 September, 1994 at Esquimalt.

A milestone was passed on 11 March 1995, when a Sea King from 443 Squadron landed on board *Regina* for the first time.

Regina's first major deployment saw her leave Esquimalt on 10 May 1995 to conduct exercises with several southeast Asian countries. During the trip, stopovers were made in Malaysia, Hong Kong, Thailand, the Philippines, Singapore, Australia, Indonesia and Western Samoa before she returned home on 4 August.

On 10 October 1995, *Regina* was in the Strait of Juan de Fuca conducting RASing operations with *Protecteur* when tragedy struck. A piece of equipment, under tension, let go and struck Leading Seaman James Hauser. He was flown to a nearby hospital, but later died.

In the spring of 1996 *Regina*, along with *Algonquin*, *Protecteur* and *Winnipeg*, sailed for the three-month exercise Westploy '96, during which, on 22 April, she called at Ho Chi Minh City, the first North American warship to do so since the end of the Vietnam war. She then rejoined her consorts to take part in Exercise Rimpac '96, off Hawaii.

Battle Honours:	Atlantic	1942-1945
	Mediterranean	1943
	Normandy	1944
	English Channel	1944-1945

The Heritage: *The first* Regina *was a corvette which joined the RCN in 1942. She was torpedoed and sunk off Cornwall on 8 August, 1944.*

TORONTO in Halifax in 1994, passing under the Angus L. Macdonald Bridge.

HMCS *Toronto (2nd)*

✪

Provisionally accepted on 23 December, 1992, in Halifax, *Toronto* was the third CPF to be handed over to the navy. She immediately began a series of trials which were to last six months.

She was formally commissioned in Toronto on 29 July, 1993, and on 24 September became the first CPF to entertain royalty, when Prince Andrew paid the ship a short visit. *Toronto* spent the rest of the year conducting combat systems trials.

Between 17 January and 15 February, 1994, she was off the coast of Virginia, conducting further trials, and on 8 April, 1994, became fully operational. On 17 May she was in Liverpool, U.K., to attend the dedication of a monument commemorating Canada's contribution to the Battle of the Atlantic. She remained in European waters to participate in the 50th Anniversary D Day observances, finally departing for Halifax on 7 June.

On August 15, *Toronto* departed Halifax to relieve HMCS *Halifax* off the coast of the former Yugoslavia on 30 August. She arrived back in Halifax on 26 January, 1995, after steaming some 24,900 miles in support of Operation Sharp Guard.

On 24 March, 1995, *Toronto* departed Halifax to relieve HMCS *Halifax* on FISHPAT off Newfoundland. On 20 April, she left Halifax again, this time heading for the Netherlands, England and Ireland to join in VE Day celebrations. After leaving, she headed for waters off Portugal to participate in the NATO exercise Linked Seas, 24 May to 6 June. She returned to Sydney, N.S. on 16 June and after a two-day visit joined Maritime Operations Group One, to participate in exercise MARCOT 1/95 off the southern coast of Nova Scotia. *Toronto* arrived back in Halifax on 30 June.

Departing Montreal on 23 August, 1995, the ship made courtesy visits to eight ports on Lake Ontario and the St. Lawrence River before reaching Montreal again on 6 September. At three of these ports, Niagara-on-the-Lake, Oakville and Port Hope, visitors were ferried to the anchored frigate.

Battle Honour:	Gulf of St.Lawrence............................ 1944

The Heritage: *The first* Toronto *was a frigate which served in the RCN 1944-1956. She was transferred to the Norwegian Navy in 1959, ending her career in 1977 under the name of* Valkyrien.

VANCOUVER leaving Halifax for Esquimalt, 18 June, 1993.

HMCS *Vancouver* (2nd)

Following builder's trials, *Vancouver* was provisionally accepted by the navy on 11 September, 1992. On 18 June, 1993, she departed Halifax for the west coast and what was to become her home port, Esquimalt.

Vancouver was commissioned in her namesake city on 23 August, 1993. She was the first CPF assigned to the Pacific fleet and the third of her class to enter service.

On 15 April, 1994, she was considered fully operational and joined the Second Canadian Destroyer Squadron. On 16 May she departed Esquimalt, along with other Canadian ships, to participate in RIMPAC '94 exercises off Hawaii. Enroute, one of her four diesel-electric generators failed, but the ship was able to continue on her mission. This was the first time a CPF had taken part in a large-scale international exercise. *Vancouver* then headed for points west of Hawaii, spending most of July on visits to ports in Japan and South Korea, promoting Canadian defence technology. She returned to Esquimalt on 5 August, 1994.

During the first part of 1995, *Vancouver*, as part of Maritime Operations Group Two, participated in an American Battle Group training exercise off southern California. During this time she also successfully fired her vertical-launched Sea Sparrow missile system for the first time.

Departing Esquimalt on 27 March, she made her first CANPAT (sovereignty patrol - showing the flag, fisheries observation, illegal logging and drug trafficking watch) along the west coast of Vancouver Island toward Prince Rupert. After a day's stopover, she returned home via the Inside Passage. During the patrol she caught one vessel fishing illegally, and two "probables".

Vancouver left Esquimalt in company with *Regina* on 10 May 1995 to conduct exercises with the ships of several southeast Asian countries. Stopovers included Tonga, Australia, New Zealand and Western Samoa, the ship returning home on 4 August.

Battle Honours:	Aleutians	1942-1943
	Atlantic	1944-1945

The Heritage: *The first* Vancouver *was a corvette which served in the RCN 1942-1945. She was broken up in 1946.*

HMCS *Ville de Québec (2nd)*

★

She was the first of the frigates completed by MIL Davie, Quebec. Builder's trials commenced in the fall of 1992, and she arrived in Halifax on 22 May, 1993. *Ville de Québec* was provisionally accepted on 23 September, 1993, in a short ceremony held at M & M Industries, Dartmouth.

In November 1993, she visited Boston, Mass., her first call at a foreign port. From 13 to 30 December 1993, she was MARCOM's "ready duty ship" (on four-hour standby for patrol, search and rescue, and drug interdiction missions), the first CPF to be so utilized. Although not yet formally commissioned, she relieved *Annapolis* in OPERATION FORWARD ACTION (the UN embargo of Haiti) on 23 April, 1994.

Early into this assignment, *Ville de Québec* carried out her first helicopter hoist transfer and her first replenishment at sea (with the oiler *USS John Lenthall*). After five days on patrol, during which she conducted 14 boardings, she was relieved by *Terra Nova*, returning to Halifax on 13 May.

On 11 June, *Ville de Québec* was on a weapons test about 29 miles southeast of Halifax, when she accidently fired four shells from her 57mm Bofors gun. One of the ship's computers had been following a towed target, but before the target was in range, the gun was accidently tripped by a crew member and automatically fired four non-explosive rounds in about one second. The rounds travelled more than 3 miles, but fortunately struck nothing.

Ville de Québec was commissioned in Quebec City on 14 July, 1994, and will be based on Halifax. She will be the first CPF with a mixed-gender crew, and French will be the working language on board.

She became "fully operational" (all trials completed and ready for any assignment) on 19 October, 1994.

VILLE DE QUÉBEC

On 9 February, 1995, she departed Halifax to take part in the NATO exercise Strong Resolve off Norway from 20 February to 10 March, returning home on 24 March.

Leaving Halifax on 5 July, *Ville de Québec* relieved *Montreal* in Agosta, Italy on 7-8 July, to become Canada's representative in NATO's Standing Naval Force Atlantic in the Adriatic Sea for the next six months. She returned to Halifax on 19 December.

In March 1996, the ship took part in the major NATO Exercise Unified Spirit off the U.S. eastern seaboard, returning to her base on 3 April.

Battle Honours:	Atlantic	1942-1944
	Gulf of St.Lawrence	1942
	Mediterranean	1943
	English Channel	1944-1945

The Heritage: *The first* Ville de Québec *was a corvette which served in the RCN 1942-1945. She was sold in 1946 for conversion to a merchant ship.*

CANADIAN PATROL FRIGATE
CITY CLASS - *MONTREAL* BATCH

Statistical Data					
Name	Pendant	Laid Down	Launched	Prov. Acc*	Commissioned
CHARLOTTETOWN	339	18/12/93	1/10/94	28/4/95	9/9/95
FREDERICTON	337	25/4/92	26/6/93	24/2/94	10/9/94
MONTREAL	336	9/2/91	26/2/92	27/7/93	21/7/94
OTTAWA	341	29/4/95	4/5/96	31/7/96	28/9/96
ST.JOHN'S	340	24/8/94	26/8/95	12/12/95	24/6/96
WINNIPEG	338	20/3/93	5/12/93	11/10/94	23/6/95

*Indicates ship became "navy" manned. For ships statistical data see *Halifax* Batch.

CHARLOTTETOWN in 1995.

HMCS *Charlottetown* (3rd)

Her keel was laid on 18 December, 1993, and she was launched and christened on 1 October, 1994.

The navy took possession of her on 28 April, 1995, in Halifax. While other ships of the City class have their speed restricted due to the *Halifax's* problems, *Charlottetown* will serve as a guinea pig to test her connecting rods during her sea trials. After 15,000 hours of running, the rods are to be closely re-examined.

The ship was commissioned on 9 September (in Charlottetown, PEI), following which, after a period in drydock at Halifax, she began workups in mid-February, 1996. On 15 March she headed south for a series of exercises preliminary to being declared fully operational on 6 May. She paid a courtesy visit to her namesake port, 26-29 May.

Battle Honours: Atlantic.. 1942
Gulf of St. Lawrence............................. 1942-1944

The Heritage: *The first* Charlottetown *was a corvette which joined the RCN in 1941. She was torpedoed and sunk in the St. Lawrence River on 11 September, 1942.*

The second Charlottetown *was a frigate which served in the RCN 1944-1947. Her hull was scuttled as a breakwater at Oyster Bay, B.C., 1948.*

HMCS *Fredericton* (2nd)

She was floated up and christened on 26 June, 1993. Following fitting-out and builder's trials, she arrived in Halifax for the first time on 24 February, 1994, and was provisionally accepted.

Fredericton was commissioned on 10 September, 1994, in Saint John, and will be based on Halifax.

She left Halifax on 9 February 1995 to attend an International Defence Exhibit held in Abu Dhabi, United Arab Emirates. *Fredericton* made stopovers in Kuwait, Oman, Saudia Arabia and Israel to demonstrate Canadian technology. On 5 April, *Fredericton* was steaming off Somalia, when she heard a distress call from the yacht *Longo Barda*, which was being attacked by pirates. When *Fredericton* arrived on the scene, the pirates fled. The yacht was then escorted to safer waters and the two vessels parted company the next day. For this action, as well as a successful tour of the Middle East, the ship was later awarded the Canadian Forces Unit Commendation. She was the first CPF to receive this award. She arrived back in Halifax on 1 May.

Fredericton spent the weekend of 30 September berthed in Saint John, N.B. after completing a week of training activities off Nova Scotia and in the Gulf of Maine. She returned to Halifax on 3 October.

On 28 November, "Freddie" departed Halifax to begin a six-month tour in the Adriatic. She spent Christmas Day at Trieste, Italy, in company with HMS *Beaver* and NRP *Corte Real* of STANAVFORLANT. From 29 February to 11 March she acted as flagship to the Force. Then, owing to a communications problem in the flagship of Standing Naval Force Mediterranean, she filled the same role for that Force, 17-19 March. It was the first time a Candian ship had filled both functions during the same deployment. *Fredericton* was home again on 4 April.

Battle Honours: Atlantic... 1942-1945

The Heritage: *The first* Fredericton *was a corvette which served in RCN 1941-1945. She was broken up in 1946.*

HMCS *Montreal* (2nd)

Montreal was provisionally accepted by the Navy on 27 July, 1993, in a short ceremony held at Halifax.

She carried out various trials over the following 23 months, and in January 1994 visited Norfolk, Virginia, for the first time. On 16 February, when she was coming alongside in Halifax, she bumped the submarine *Okanagan*. Damage to the frigate was minimal, while the sub received a cracked sonar dome.

She was commissioned in Montreal on 21 July, 1994, and will be a French-language vessel operating out of Halifax. The fifth Canadian Patrol Frigate to do so, she became fully operational on 19 October, 1994.

She departed Halifax on 4 January, 1995 to join NATO's Standing Naval Force Atlantic in the Adriatic Sea off the former Yugoslavia. After a short delay outside Halifax to effect minor repairs to her desalination units and pick up her Sea King (delayed due to weather), she proceeded to Cartagena, Spain where she relieved *Halifax* on 16 January. She completed seven patrols during which she conducted 57 boardings, diverted four ships and acted as STANAVFORLANT flagship on two separate occasions. She arrived back in Halifax on 19 July.

Battle Honours:	Atlantic	1944-1945

The Heritage: *The first* Montreal *was a frigate which served in the RCN 1943-1945. She was broken up in 1947.*

HMCS *Ottawa* (4th)

Steel cutting for this ship was begun in September 1993. Her keel was laid 29 April, 1995. After commissioning, scheduled for June 1997, she is expected to operate out of Esquimalt.

She was scheduled to be commissioned at Cornwall, Ont., 28 Sept., 1996.

Battle Honours:	Atlantic	1939-1945
	Normandy	1944
	English Channel	1944
	Biscay	1944

The Heritage: *The first* Ottawa *was a destroyer, the former HMS* Crusader, *which joined the RCN in 1938. She was torpedoed and sunk in the North Atlantic on 13 September, 1942.*

The second Ottawa *was also a destroyer, the former HMS* Griffin, *which served in the RCN 1943-1945. She was broken up in 1946.*

The third Ottawa *was a destroyer/helicopter carrier which served in the RCN 1956-1992.*

HMCS *St. John's*

The first ship of the name, her keel was laid on 24 August, 1994, and she will operate out of Halifax after commissioning, which is scheduled for 24 June, 1996, in St. John's, Newfoundland.

The ship was delivered to the Navy on 12 December, 1995, and spent the following six months on pre-commissioning trials.

MONTREAL in 1993

WINNIPEG arriving at Esquimalt, 17 February, 1995.

HMCS *Winnipeg* (2nd)

Winnipeg was the first CPF to have her engine room module units completed at the Georgetown, P.E.I. shipyard and barged around to Saint John, where they arrived in October, 1992.

She was floated up on 5 December, 1993, christened on 25 June, 1994 in Saint John, N.B., and delivered to the navy on 11 October. *Winnipeg* left Halifax on 16 January, 1995, and after stops in Aruba, Puerto Vallarta and San Diego, arrived in Esquimalt on 17 February. She was commissioned there on 23 June, 1995, and joined Maritime Operations Group 2 on 16 October.

In the spring of 1996, along with *Algonquin*, *Protecteur* and *Regina*, she took part in the three-month exercise Westploy '96 and, afterward, in Rimpac '96 off Hawaii.

Battle Honours: Atlantic.. 1943-1945

The Heritage: *The first* Winnipeg *was an Algerine class minesweeper which served in the RCN 1943-1946. Transferred to the Belgian Navy in 1959, she served until 1966 as* A.F. Dufour.

Appendix 1				
Ships that took part in OPERATION SHARP GUARD				
UN sanctions against Yugoslavia				
Ship	Leave Halifax	Join SNFA	Leave SNFA	Arrive Halifax
ALGONQUIN[1]	29/3/93	24/6/93	***	15/10/93
IROQUOIS [2]	25/9/93	?/10/93	15/4/94	25/4/94
PRESERVER	27/1/94	10/2/94	***	14/6/94
HALIFAX	2/4/94	15/4/94	30/8/94	9/9/94
TORONTO[3]	15/8/94	30/8/94	16/1/95	26/1/95
MONTREAL[4]	4/1/95	16/1/95	8/7/95	19/7/95
PRESERVER	5/7/95	***	***	30/6/95
VILLE DE QUÈBEC	26/6/95	7/7/95	17/12/95	19/12/95
FREDERICTON	28/11/95	14/12/95	***	4/4/96
HALIFAX	18/3/96	***	***	***

1 - Left Halifax to join the NATO Fleet; the fleet was then deployed to the Adriatic and arrived there June 24/93 to enforce UN sanctions against the former Yugoslavia. During the deployment, *Algonquin* conducted 88 boardings.

2 - During deployment, *Iroquois* conducted 98 boardings.

3 - During deployment, *Toronto* conducted 370 hailings, 56 boardings and 25 diversions.

4 - During deployment, *Montreal* conducted 187 hailings, 57 boardings and 4 diversions.

***Information unavailable

	Appendix 2			
	Ships that took part in OPERATION FORWARD ACTION			
	UN Sanctions against Haiti			
Ship	Leave Hfx/Esq	Arrive Haiti	Leave Haiti	Arrive Hfx/Esq
PRESERVER	28/9/93	18/10/93	***	23/11/93
GATINEAU	28/9/93	18/10/93	***	23/11/93
FRASER	28/9/93	18/10/93	17/12/93	23/12/93
PROVIDER [1]	1/12/93E	17/12/93	13/1/94	3/94E
FRASER[2]	8/1/94	13/1/94	25/3/94	31/3/94
ANNAPOLIS	10/3/94E	25/3/94	23/4/94	***
VILLE DE QUÈBEC[3]	***	23/4/94	28/4/94	13/5/94
TERRA NOVA[4]	5/4/94	28/4/94	13/7/94	18/7/94
KOOTENAY	21/6/94E	13/7/94	15/9/94	***
TERRA NOVA	7/9/94	15/9/94	29/9/94	19/10/94

1 - Conducted exercises in Atlantic with other Canadian units after leaving Haiti.

2 - On *Fraser's* two tours, she conducted 73 boardings and 450 hailings while spending a total of 134 days on station.

3 - *Ville de Québec* conducted 14 boardings during her 5 days on patrol.

4 - *Terra Nova* spent 87 days at sea and upon her departure, completed her 90th boarding. On 5 July, she rescued 67 occupants of one boat, and on 8 July, 57 occupants of another.

  Canada's contribution to the naval blockade of Haiti ended on 1 October, 1994, when *Terra Nova* departed. (The country had by then been peacefully occupied by an American force.) Overall, Canadian personnel conducted 9,424 hailings and 1,388 armed boardings, and diverted 119 ships. This was 19% of all UN hailings, 18% of boardings and 13% of diversions.

*** Information unavailable

Appendix 3

1. Conversions / Major Refit Schedules

St. Laurent Class / Conversion to helicopter carrying ship

Ship	Start	Finish	Where Done
ASSINIBOINE	6/62	28/6/63	Victoria Machinery, Victoria B.C.
FRASER	2/7/65	22/10/66	Canadian Vickers, Montreal, Que
MARGAREE	29/9/64	15/10/65	Victoria Machinery, Victoria B.C.
OTTAWA	6/63	21/10/64	Victoria Machinery, Victoria B.C.
SKEENA	7/64	14/8/65	Davie Shipbuilding, Lauzon, Que.
ST. LAURENT	***	4/10/63	Burrard Drydock, Vancouver, B.C.

2.DELEX Refits

Ship	Start	Finish	Where Done
ASSINIBOINE	23/4/79	16/11/79	Vickers, Montreal
FRASER	19/10/81	28/5/82	Vickers, Montreal
MARGAREE	5/5/80	28/11/80	Vickers, Montreal*
OTTAWA	19/4/82	26/11/82	Vickers, Montreal
SAGUENAY	29/10/79	23/5/80	Vickers, Montreal
SKEENA	12/4/81	20/11/81	Vickers, Montreal
GATINEAU	9/81	12/11/82	Ship Repair Unit-Pacific, Esquimalt
KOOTENAY	25/10/82	21/10/83	Halifax Shipyards
RESTIGOUCHE	3/12/84	29/11/85	Ship Repair Unit-Pacific, Esquimalt
TERRA NOVA	21/11/83	9/11/84	Ship Repair Unit-Pacific, Esquimalt
MACKENZIE	26/5/86	16/1/87	Burrard Yarrow at CFB Esquimalt
QU'APPELLE	25/5/83	13/1/84	Burrard Yarrow at CFB Esquimalt
SASKATCHEWAN	27/5/85	17/6/86	Burrard Yarrow at CFB Esquimalt
YUKON	28/5/84	16/1/85	Burrard Yarrow at CFB Esquimalt
ANNAPOLIS	19/8/85	15/9/86	Saint John Shipbuilding, Saint John
NIPIGON	27/6/83	22/8/84	Davie Shipbuilding, Lauzon

* Work completed by Ship Repair Unit, Halifax, the following summer. *** Information unavailable

3. TRUMP Refits		
Ship	Start	Finish
ALGONQUIN	26/10/87	11/10/91
ATHABASKAN	10/91	4/6/94
HURON	7/93	25/11/94
IROQUOIS	1/11/89	3/7/92

All the work was done at MIL Davie, Lauzon, Que.

COMMANDING OFFICERS

Algonquin (2nd)

CDR R.L. McClean, RCN	3/11/73 - 7/5/76
CDR H.M.D. MacNeil, RCN	8/5/76 - 10/8/77
CDR J. Harwood, RCN	11/8/77 - 19/3/78
CDR L.C.A. Westrop, RCN	20/3/78 - 24/7/80
CDR D.E. Pollard	25/7/80 - 10/4/82
CDR A.J. Goode	10/4/82 - 17/12/83
CDR K.J. Summers	17/12/83 - 1/7/85
CDR J.C.A. Nadeau	1/7/85 - 10/8/87
LCDR J.G.V. Tremblay	10/8/87 - 6/4/88
LCDR J.A.P. Lebel	30/6/88 - 15/7/89
CDR J.Y. Forcier	17/7/89 - 15/7/93
CDR P.C. Leblanc	15/7/93 - 29/3/94
CDR J.B. McCarthy	29/3/94 - 15/7/95
CDR A.W. Round	15/7/95 -

Annapolis (2nd)

CDR R.C.K. Peers, RCN	19/12/64 - 6/9/66
CDR D.N. Mainguy, RCN	6/9/66 - 18/12/67
CDR D. Ross, RCN	4/1/68 - 21/8/69
CDR A.G. Lowe	21/8/69 - 20/2/71
CDR A.P. Campbell	1/4/71 - 8/9/72
CDR J. Dent	8/9/72 - 18/7/75
CDR R.A. Willson	8/8/75 - 14/5/77
CDR A.R.H. Wood	14/5/77 - 16/4/79
CDR W.P. Dumbrille	16/4/79 - 1/10/80
CDR J.C. Braconnier	1/10/80 - 28/6/82
CDR J.C. Bain	28/6/82 - 23/4/84
CDR G.O. Hurford	23/4/84 - 1/8/85
LCDR R.J. Kerr	1/8/85 - 16/12/85
LCDR D.G. McNeil	16/12/85 - 26/7/86
CDR B.F. Beaudry	26/7/86 - 4/7/88
CDR R.J. Neveu	4/7/88 - 28/9/89
CDR A.L. Vey	28/9/89 - 27/9/90
CDR J.D. Fraser	27/9/90 - 25/1/91
CDR R.R. Town	25/1/91 - 26/7/93
CDR S.C. Bertrand	26/7/93 - 6/1/95
CDR D.W. Robertson	6/1/95 -

Assiniboine (2nd)

CDR E.P. Earnshaw, RCN	16/8/56 - 23/5/58
CDR J.R. Coulter, RCN	24/5/58 - 19/2/59
CAPT J.C. Pratt, RCN	19/2/59 - 17/8/60
CAPT J.A. Charles, RCN	17/8/60 - 18/6/61
CDR V. Browne, RCN	18/8/61 - 30/4/62
CDR E.A. Wiggs, RCN	30/4/62 - 22/6/62
CDR W.S. Blandy, RCN	28/6/62 - 15/1/66
CDR T.L. Hebbert, RCN	15/1/66 - 15/7/67
CDR G.L. Edwards, RCN	15/7/67 - 6/7/70
LCDR E. Cullwick	6/7/70 - 18/8/70
CDR L.J. Cavan	18/8/70 - 10/1/72
LCDR H. Kieran	10/1/72 - 17/7/72
CDR T.S. Hayward	17/7/72 - 20/11/72
CDR G.G. Freill	20/11/72 - 22/12/72
LCDR R. Thomas	22/12/72 - 14/4/73
CDR R. Corneil	14/4/73 - 20/5/74
CDR R. Thomas	20/5/74 - 10/6/74
CDR M. Taylor	10/6/74 - 16/7/75
CDR E.K. Kelly	16/7/75 - 27/6/77
CDR M. Duncan	27/6/77 - 31/7/79
CDR G. Braithwaite	31/7/79 - 10/8/81
CDR R. Moore	10/8/81 - 4/7/83
CDR W.G. Lund	4/7/83 - 1/6/84
CDR R.M. Bernard	1/6/84 - 1/8/85
CDR B.D. Neal	1/8/85 - 11/6/87
CDR D.G. McNeil	11/6/87 - 2/1/89

Athabaskan (3rd)

CDR R.D. Yanow	30/9/72 - 6/9/74
CDR G.L. Edwards	6/9/74 - 29/3/76
CDR J.C. Slade	29/3/76 - 7/7/78
CDR J.B. O'Reilly	7/7/78 - 7/7/80
CDR J.W. McIntosh	7/7/80 - 2/8/81
CDR K.R. Scotten	2/8/81 - 31/3/84
CDR D. Cogdon	31/3/84 - 16/5/86
CDR G.R. Maddison	16/5/86 - 14/4/88
CDR J.D. Peacocke	14/4/88 - 11/7/90
CDR K.J. Pickford	11/7/90 - 6/9/91
LCDR A.G. Munroe	6/9/91 - 9/7/92
LCDR J.G. King	9/7/92 - 29/3/94

CDR P.C. Leblanc	29/3/94 -

Calgary (2nd)

CDR G.A. Paulson	21/2/94 -

Charlottetown (2nd)

CDR M.A. Wylie	29/7/94 -

Chaudière (2nd)

CDR V.J. Wilgress, RCN	14/11/59 - 25/4/61
CDR P.J. Pratley, RCN	24/4/61 - 11/4/63
CDR R.H. Falls, RCN	11/4/63 - 25/8/64
CDR G.R. Macfarlane, RCN	25/8/64 - 17/1/66
CDR J.I. Manore, RCN	17/1/66 - 26/8/67
LCDR W.G. Brown, RCN	26/8/67 - 24/11/67
LCDR J.L. Woodbury, RCN	24/11/67 - 8/12/67
CDR P.J. Bissell, RCN	8/12/67 - 20/1/70
CDR H. Rusk	20/1/70 - 30/6/71
LCDR D.R. Donaldson	30/6/71 - 23/5/73
LCDR J.G. Comeau	24/5/73 - 23/5/74

Columbia (2nd)

CDR W.P. Hayes, RCN	7/11/59 - 25/4/61
CDR D.W. Knox, RCN	25/4/61 - 4/9/64
CDR P.R. Hinton, RCN	4/9/64 - 15/9/65
CDR A.C. McMillin, RCN	15/9/65 - 20/2/67
CDR R.D. Okros, RCN	20/2/67 - 31/8/68
CDR T.C. Shuckburg, RCN	31/8/68 - 23/7/70
CDR E.A. Makin	23/7/70 - 6/8/72
CDR R.F. Choat	7/8/72 - 18/2/74

Fraser (2nd)

CDR R. Phillips, RCN	28/6/57 - 3/1/59
CDR D.L. MacKnight, RCN	3/1/59 - 4/1/61
CDR D.J. Sheppard, RCN	4/1/61 - 6/9/62
CAPT G.H. Hayes, RCN	6/9/62 - 3/10/62
CDR R.C. Thurber, RCN	3/10/62 - 5/8/64
CDR R. Carle, RCN	5/8/64 - 2/7/65
CDR J.F. Watson, RCN	22/10/66 - 4/7/68
CDR F.W. Crickard, RCN	4/7/68 - 17/11/69
CDR R.G. Guy	17/11/69 - 30/6/71
CDR C.M. Thomas	30/6/71 - 12/4/73

CDR L.I. MacDonald	11/3/74 - 15/8/76
CDR P.W. Cairns	15/8/76 - 12/8/77
CDR H.R. Waddell	12/8/77 - 18/12/78
CDR J.B. Elson	18/12/78 - 26/1/81
CDR J. Nethercott	26/1/81 - 1/5/82
CDR W.B. Hodgkin	1/5/82 - 12/12/83
CDR V.U. Auns	12/12/83 - 16/8/85
CDR B.M. Power	16/8/85 - 4/7/88
CDR I.G. Parker	4/7/88 - 19/7/90
CDR J.A.Y. Plante	19/7/90 - 19/12/90
CDR H.W. McEwen	19/12/90 - 10/5/91
CDR E.P. Webster	10/5/91 - 23/7/93
CDR H.R. Smith	23/7/93 - 30/9/94

Fredericton (2nd)

CDR D.J. Gallina	20/9/93 - 7/7/95
CDR K.D.W. Laing	7/7/95 -

Gatineau (2nd)

CAPT H.L. Quinn, DSC, RCN	17/2/59 -14/9/59
CAPT F.B. Caldwell, RCN	15/9/59 - 27/1/61
LCDR R.A. Shimmin, RCN	28/1/61 - 24/5/61
LCDR H.C. Mecredy, RCN	25/5/61 - 24/8/61
CDR A.H. McDonald, RCN	25/8/61 - 21/8/62
CDR J.W. Roberts, RCN	22/8/62 - 28/4/64
CDR W.G. Kinsman, DSO, RCN	29/4/64 - 11/8/65
CDR J.A. Fulton, RCN	12/8/65 - 8/9/66
CDR W.A. Hughes, RCN	8/9/66 - 29/9/69
CDR T.S. Murphy	14/4/71 - 3/7/71
CDR J.C. Slade	3/7/71 - 11/7/75
CDR L.G. Temple	11/7/75 - 11/11/77
CDR J.B. McKenzie	11/11/77 - 26/7/79
CDR C.D.E. Cronk	26/7/79 - 11/6/81
CDR D.M. Robison	11/6/81 - 4/7/83
CDR T.C. Heath	4/7/83 - 1/8/85
CDR J.A. Keenliside	1/8/85 - 21/4/87
CDR G. Jeffries	21/4/87 - 4/7/88
CDR A.E. Tanguay	4/7/88 - 7/7/90
CDR R.H. Edwards	7/7/90 - 10/7/92
CDR R.G. Allen	10/7/92 - 14/1/94
CDR J.A. Westlake	14/1/94 - 28/7/95
CDR D.O. Thamer	28/7/95 -

Halifax (2nd)

CDR R.I. Clayton	1/5/89 - 21/12/92
CDR G.B. Burke	21/12/92 - 24/10/94
CDR L.D. Sweeney	24/10/94 -

Huron (2nd)

CDR R.J. Hitesman	14/12/72 - 25/7/75
CDR L.J. Cavan	25/7/75 - 15/7/77
CDR M.H.D. Taylor	15/7/77 - 22/7/78
CDR J.D. Spalding	22/7/78 - 24/7/81
CDR R.J. Deluca	24/7/81 - 14/1/83
CDR G.L. Garnett	14/1/83 - 2/7/84
CDR J.A. King	2/7/84 - 6/1/87
CDR G.G. Jeffrey	6/1/87 - 21/4/87
CDR J.A. Keenliside	21/4/87 - 22/7/88
CDR D.E. Collinson	22/7/88 - 3/8/90
CDR R.H. Melnick	8/8/90 - 25/6/91
CDR G.A. Paulson	25/6/91 - 27/9/91
CDR F. Scherber	27/9/91 - 24/4/92
CDR G.A. Paulson	24/4/92 - 29/6/92
CDR G.B. McCarthy	1/5/93 - 29/3/94
CDR R.C. Lelonde	29/3/94 - 29/7/94
CDR R.A. Maze	29/7/94 -

Iroquois (2nd)

CDR D.N. MacGillivray	29/7/72 - 24/3/75
CDR G.G. Freill	24/3/75 - 4/5/77
CDR R.E. George	4/5/77 - 30/6/79
CDR E.K. Kelly	1/7/99 - 16/4/81
CDR L.G. Mason	16/4/81 - 30/6/82
CDR G.L. Garnett	30/6/82 - 13/1/83
CDR L.E. Murray	18/4/83 - 4/1/85
CDR B.R. Brown	4/1/85 - 25/6/86
CDR P. Ballard	25/6/86 - 10/10/88
CDR G. Romanow	15/7/90 - 5/8/91
CDR L.J. Edmunds	5/8/91 - 15/7/94
CDR R. Girouard	15/7/94 -

Kootenay (2nd)

CDR R.J. Pickford, RCN	7/3/59 - 11/7/60
CDR H. Shorten, RCN	11/7/60 - 19/9/62
CDR D.H. Ryan, RCN	19/9/62 - 15/1/65
CDR C.G. Pratt, RCN	15/1/65 - 1/6/66
CDR W.P. Rikely, RCN	1/6/66 - 1/7/67

CDR G.C. McMorris, RCN	1/7/67 - 15/11/68
CDR M Tremblay, RCN	15/11/68 - 21/3/69
CDR N. St.C. Norman	21/3/69 - 14/1/70
CDR J.L. Creech	12/1/72 - 17/2/73
CDR R.H. Kirby	17/2/73 - 14/6/74
CDR J. Spalding	14/6/74 - 16/7/76
CDR B.P. Moore	16/7/76 - 27/6/78
CDR B. Johnston	27/6/78 - 11/8/80
CDR B.H. Beckett	11/8/80 - 28/6/82
CDR S.K. Jessen	28/6/82 - 9/1/83
CDR P.C. Young	24/1/84 - 5/7/85
CDR B.R. Melville	5/7/85 - 30/7/87
CDR J. Dickson	30/7/87 - 21/7/89
CDR J.D. Fraser	21/7/91 - 29/5/92
CDR M.R. Bellows	29/5/92 - 31/7/92
CDR D.J. Kyle	31/7/92 - 30/6/94
CDR R.H. Dawe	30/6/94 -

Mackenzie

CDR A.B. German, RCN	6/10/62 - 29/5/64
CDR H.J. Wade, RCN	29/5/64 - 17/1/66
LCDR R.D. Okros, RCN	17/1/66 - 7/3/66
CDR G.M. De Rosenroll, RCN	7/3/66 - 11/8/67
LCDR W.J. Draper, RCN	11/8/67 - 22/11/67
CDR O.J. Cavenaugh, RCN	22/11/67 - 24/7/69
CDR R.L. McLean	24/7/69 - 20/1/71
CDR G.G. Armstrong	20/1/71 - 6/8/72
LCDR R.J. Deluca	6/8/72 - 11/9/72
CDR R.H. Kirby	11/9/72 - 23/1/73
CDR R.D.C. Sweeny	23/1/73 - 17/9/74
CDR R.L. Donaldson	17/9/74 - 21/5/76
CDR J. Chouinard	21/5/76 - 14/1/77
CDR J.W. McIntosh	14/1/77 - 31/12/78
CDR H.R. Waddell	31/12/78 - 27/8/81
CDR T.C. Milne	27/8/81 - 19/12/83
CDR J. Nethercott	19/12/83 - 1/8/85
CDR K.A. Nason	1/8/85 - 25/4/86
CDR A.J. Hollington-Sawyer	15/9/86 - 9/7/88
CDR R.W. Bowers	9/7/88 - 20/7/90
CDR R.P. Harrison	20/7/90 - 4/1/93
CDR J.P. Lebel	4/1/93 - 30/7/93

Margaree (2nd)

CDR J.E. Korning, RCN	5/10/57 - 10/11/59

CDR E.V.P. Sunderland, RCN	10/11/59 - 17/8/60
CDR J.H. Maclean, RCN	17/8/60 - 22/5/62
CDR J.L. Panabaker, RCN	22/5/62 - 26/9/64
CDR R.C. MacLean, RCN	15/10/65 - 3/7/67
CDR P.M. Birch-Jones, RCN	4/7/67 - 23/8/68
CDR R.I. Hitesman, RCN	23/8/68 - 25/7/70
CDR J.K. Kennedy	25/7/70 - 24/1/72
LCDR D. Nugent	24/1/72 - 5/4/72
CDR R.G. Campbell	5/4/72 - 4/1/74
CDR R.E. George	4/1/74 - 18/12/75
CDR R.J. Lancashire	18/12/75 - 10/8/77
CDR P.W. Cairns	10/8/77 - 13/7/78
CDR R.A. Rutherford	13/7/78 - 12/8/80
CDR P.J. Stow	12/8/80 - 29/5/82
CDR R.W. Allen	29/5/82 - 1/4/84
CDR J.M. Ewan	1/4/84 - 1/1/86
CDR A.E. Delamere	1/1/86 - 4/1/88
CDR T.N. Brockway	4/1/88 - 6/7/89
CDR G.G. Borgal	6/7/89 - 17/12/91
CDR D.O. Thamer	17/12/91 - 2/5/92

Montreal (2nd)

CDR S.D. Andrews	31/3/93 - 28/6/93
CDR C.D. Gunn	28/6/93 - 21/7/95
CDR D.W. Shubaly	21/7/95 -

Nipigon (2nd)

CDR D.R. Saxon, DSC, RCN	30/5/64 - 19/5/66
CDR J.B. Carling, RCN	19/5/66 - 11/9/67
CDR R.F. Choat, RCN	11/9/67 - 19/12/68
LCDR O.S. Chorneyko, RCN	19/12/68 - 4/2/69
CDR R.C. Brown, RCN	4/2/69 - 31/8/70
LCDR L.I. MacDonald	31/8/70 - 29/9/70
CDR A.H. Brookbank	29/9/70 - 19/6/72
CDR D.A. Avery	19/6/72 - 10/4/74
CDR J.D. Sine	10/4/74 - 23/5/75
CDR F.H. Hope	23/5/75 - 1/9/76
CDR H.L. Davies	1/9/76 - 15/5/78
CDR R.C. Waller	15/5/78 - 12/6/80
CDR D.E. Gibb	12/6/80 - 19/7/82
CDR W.G. Lund	19/7/82 - 2/4/84
CDR H.W. Hendel	2/4/84 - 15/7/86
CDR D.E. Miller	15/7/86 - 5/10/87
CDR E.J. Lerhe	5/10/87 - 6/1/89

CDR M.A. Wylie	6/1/89 - 12/7/89
CDR S.C. Doucette	12/7/89 - 21/6/91
CDR K.S. White	21/6/91 - 26/7/93
CDR J.A. Westlake	26/7/93 - 4/1/94
LCDR E.P. DesLauriers	4/1/94 - 2/5/94
CDR M.P. Palmer	2/5/94 -

Ottawa (3rd)

CDR C.R. Parker, DSC, RCN	10/11/56 - 7/7/58
CDR W.H. Willson, DSC, RCN	7/7/58 - 28/4/59
CDR I.B. Morrow, RCN	28/4/59 - 19/8/61
LCDR I.A. MacPherson, RCN	19/8/61 - 25/3/63
CDR T.C. Shuckburg, RCN	25/3/63 -
CDR J.P. Cote, RCN	28/10/64 - 28/7/67
CDR C. Cotaras, RCN	28/7/67 - 15/7/68
CDR P. Simard, RCN	15/7/68 - 15/5/70
CDR M.H. Tremblay	15/5/70 - 7/2/72
LCDR N. Boivin	7/2/72 - 5/6/73
LCDR R.L. Burnip	5/6/73 - 14/6/74
LCDR T.C. Milne	14/6/74 - 30/8/74
CDR W.J. Draper	30/8/74 - 6/1/77
CDR L.C.A. Westrop	6/1/77 - 23/1/78
CDR J.E.D. Bell	23/1/78 - 4/7/80
CDR E.J.M. Young	4/7/80 - 10/9/82
CDR R.A.M. Burton	10/9/82 - 9/7/84
CDR K.C.E. Beardmore	9/7/84 - 11/7/86
CDR A.B. Dunlop	11/7/86 - 5/8/88
CDR M.A. Pulchny	5/8/88 - 11/7/90
CDR A.G.D. Perusse	11/7/90 - 31/7/92

Ottawa (4th)

CDR J.C.G. Goulet	5/1/96 -

Qu'Appelle (2nd)

CDR A.G. Kilpatrick, RCN	14/9/63 - 28/8/65
CDR H.D. Joy, RCN	28/8/65 - 16/1/67
CDR R. Ratcliffe, RCN	16/1/67 - 16/12/68
CDR J. Allan	16/12/68 - 28/7/70
CDR J. Rodocanachi	28/7/70 - 8/5/72
CDR R.D.C. Sweeny	8/5/72 - 22/1/73
CDR J.L. Creech	22/1/73 - 2/7/73
CDR J.D. Sine	2/7/73 - 14/2/74
CDR R.F. Choat	14/2/74 - 19/9/75
CDR K.M. Young	19/9/75 - 4/8/76

CDR R.H. Kirby	4/8/76 - 25/1/77
CDR J.M. Chouinard	25/1/77 - 4/10/78
CDR J.J. Drent	4/10/78 - 28/7/80
CDR R.J. Luke	28/7/80 - 12/7/82
CDR H.L. Davies	12/7/82 - 11/7/83
CDR J.M. Bishop	11/7/83 - 1/6/85
CDR D.J. McLean	1/6/85 - 24/4/86
LCDR W.J. Poole	24/4/86 - 1/8/86
CDR D.C. Beresford-Green	1/8/86 - 20/6/88
CDR W. Johnston	20/6/88 - 13/7/90
CDR J.G.V. Tremblay	13/7/90 - 15/7/91
CDR B.F. Lofthouse	15/7/91 - 31/7/92

Regina (2nd)

CDR M.H. Jellinek	28/6/93 - 7/8/95
CDR T.H.W. Pile	7/8/95 -

Restigouche (2nd)

CDR J.W. McDowall, RCN	7/6/58 - 4/8/60
CDR W.W. MacColl, RCN	4/8/60 - 8/8/62
CDR B.C. Thillaye, RCN	8/8/62 - 19/5/65
CDR H.W. Vondette, RCN	19/5/65 - 10/8/66
CDR R.A. Evans, RCN	10/8/66 - 3/1/68
CDR P.L. McCulloch, RCN	3/1/68 - 3/8/70
CDR R.H. Kirby	12/5/72 - 7/9/72
LCDR R.C. Burnip	7/9/72 - 2/4/73
CDR R.J. Deluca	2/4/73 - 15/7/75
CDR C.J. Crowe	15/7/75 - 27/1/77
CDR R.G. Balfour	27/1/77 - 27/3/77
CDR C.J. Crowe	27/3/77 - 29/4/77
CDR H.T. Porter	29/4/77 - 29/7/78
CDR J.R. Anderson	29/7/78 - 29/9/80
CDR D.A. Henderson	29/9/80 - 10/1/83
CDR S.K. Jessen	10/1/83 - 6/7/84
CDR H.C. Silvestor	6/7/84 - 7/7/87
CDR R.D. Buck	7/7/87 - 9/3/89
CDR B.E. Mathews	9/3/89 - 19/6/89
CDR G.C. Oakley	19/6/89 - 23/8/91
CDR D. Baltes	23/8/91 - 4/1/93
CDR R.K. Taylor	4/1/93 - 29/7/94

Saguenay (2nd)

CDR G.H. Hayes, DSC, RCN	15/12/56 - 13/3/58
CDR J.H.G. Bovey, DSC, RCN	31/3/58 - 2/3/59

CDR D.S. Boyle, RCN — 2/3/59 - 14/10/59
CDR E.M. Chadwick, RCN — 14/10/59 - 23/8/61
CDR H.R. Tilley, RCN — 23/8/61 - 22/8/63
CDR H.H. Plant, RCN — 14/5/65 - 13/7/66
CDR D.A. Avery, RCN — 13/7/66 - 23/8/67
LCDR L.A. Dzioba, RCN — 23/8/67 - 15/12/67
CAPT D.H.P. Ryan, RCN — 15/12/67 - 23/1/69
CDR R. Yanow — 23/1/69 - 13/8/70
LCDR R. Hardy — 13/8/70 - 1/11/70
CDR K.M. Young — 1/11/70 -
CDR D. MacNeil — 18/7/72 - 17/6/74
CDR J. Harwood — 17/6/74 - 10/1/75
CDR J. Luke — 10/1/75 - 18/1/77
CDR C. Milne — 18/1/77 - 4/8/78
CDR J. Goode — 4/8/78 - 18/4/80
CDR A.G. Schwartz — 18/4/80 - 24/7/82
CDR E.E. Davie — 24/7/82 - 18/7/83
CDR J.M. Barlow — 18/7/83 - 17/7/85
CDR R.D. Buck — 7/7/87 - 9/3/89
CDR B.E. Mathews — 9/3/89 - 19/6/89
CDR G.C. Oakley — 19/6/89 - 23/8/91
CDR D. Baltes — 23/8/91 - 4/1/93
CDR R.K. Taylor — 4/1/93 - 29/7/94

St. Croix (2nd)

CDR K.H. Boggild, RCN — 4/10/58 - 28/5/59
CDR W.S.T. McCully, RCN — 28/5/59 - 14/3/61
CDR T.E. Connors, RCN — 14/3/61 - 22/7/62
CDR D.C. Rutherford, RCN — 22/7/62 - 31/5/63
CDR D.M. Maclennan, RCN — 31/5/53 - 4/5/64
CDR J.S. Hertzberg, RCN — 4/5/64 - 21/9/66
CDR J.I. Donald, RCN — 21/9/66 - 15/7/68
CDR J.M. Cumming, RCN — 15/7/68 - 31/8/71
LCDR R.L. Donaldson — 31/8/71 - 2/7/73
CDR T.S. Murphy — 2/7/73 - 9/9/74
CDR P.E. Simard — 9/9/74 - 15/11/74

St. John's

CDR R.S. Edwards — 29/7/94 -

St. Laurent (2nd)

CDR R.W. Timbrell, DSC, RCN — 29/10/55 - 23/1/57
CAPT A.G. Boulton, DSC, RCN — 23/1/57 - 15/3/58
CAPT H.L. Quinn, DSC, RCN — 15/3/58 - 9/1/59

LCDR E. Petley-Jones, RCN — 9/1/59 - 2/3/59
CDR M.H.E. Page, RCN — 2/3/59 - 29/6/60
CDR J.B. Fotheringham, RCN — 29/6/60 - 10/62
CDR D.D. Lee, RCN — 4/10/63 - 15/9/65
CDR W.J. Walton, RCN — 15/9/65 - 2/2/67
LCDR B. Hayes, RCN — 2/2/67 - 25/8/67
CDR M. Barrow, RCN — 25/8/67 - 11/8/69
CDR S.W. Riddell — 11/8/69 - 7/71
CDR G.G. Freill — 7/71 - 11/72
LCDR R.L. Burnip — 11/72 - 14/6/74

Saskatchewan (2nd)

CDR M.W. Mayo, RCN — 16/2/63 - 18/12/64
CDR M.A. Turner, RCN — 18/12/64 - 7/3/66
CDR P.J. Traves, RCN — 7/3/66 - 15/7/67
CDR N.S. Jackson, RCN — 15/7/67 - 23/9/68
CDR H. Rusk, RCN — 23/9/68 - 15/1/70
CDR N. St.C. Norton — 15/1/70 - 9/3/71
LCDR A. Bajkov — 9/3/71 - 2/4/71
CDR R.F. Gladman — 2/4/71 - 6/7/72
CDR T.S. Hayward — 6/7/72 - 9/4/73
CDR H.L. Davies — 9/4/73 - 31/7/73
CDR J. Harwood — 31/7/73 - 24/5/74
CDR J.G. Comeau — 24/5/74 - 1/9/76
CDR F. Hope — 1/9/76 - 3/8/78
CDR H.T. Porter — 3/8/78 - 3/7/80
CDR J.D. Sine — 3/7/80 - 5/8/82
CDR G.J. Eldridge — 19/8/82 - 25/6/84
CDR D.R.A. McLean — 25/6/84 - 15/6/85
CDR S.F. Verran — 15/6/85 - 25/7/88
CDR D.V. Adamthwaite — 25/7/88 - 15/8/90
CDR S.E. King — 15/8/90 - 21/7/92
CDR N.R. Sorsdahl — 21/7/92 - 30/4/94

Skeena (2nd)

CDR J.P.T. Dawson, RCN — 30/3/57 - 20/8/58
CDR W.M. Kidd, RCN — 20/8/58 - 1/10/59
LCDR G.M. DeRosenroll, RCN — 20/8/58 - 5/1/60
CDR T.H. Crone, RCN — 5/1/60 - 22/2/60
CDR A.L. Collier, RCN — 22/2/60 - 11/1/62
CDR R.M. Leit, RCN — 22/1/62 - 10/5/63
CDR M.A. Martin, RCN — 10/5/63 - 26/7/64
CDR C.J. Mair, RCN — 14/8/65 - 29/8/66
LCDR K.D. Lewis, RCN — 29/8/66 - 27/1/68

LT B. Elson, RCN — 27/1/68 - 16/4/68
LCDR W.G. Brown, RCN — 16/4/68 - 23/6/69
LCDR R. Dougan — 23/6/69 - 11/8/69
CDR R.L. Hughes — 11/8/69 - 23/7/70
CDR F.J. Mifflin — 23/7/70 - 5/7/72
CDR N.R. Boivin — 15/6/73 - 5/9/75
CDR J. Chouinard — 5/9/75 - 13/5/76
CDR D.E. Pollard — 13/5/76 - 29/5/78
CDR B.E. Derible — 29/5/78 - 7/7/80
CDR J.G.R. Boucher — 7/7/80 - 26/9/83
CDR I. Foldesi — 26/9/83 - 1/8/85
CDR P.J. Yans — 1/8/85 - 15/7/87
CDR D.C. Morse — 15/7/87 - 9/1/89
CDR D. MacKay — 9/1/89 - 15/7/91
CDR J.A.C. Gauthier — 15/7/91 - 15/12/91
CDR J.J. Gauvin — 15/12/91 - 26/7/93

Terra Nova

CDR W.H. Willson, DSC, RCN — 6/6/59 - 22/6/60
CDR C.G. Smith, RCN — 22/6/60 - 18/9/62
CDR J.B. Young, RCN — 18/9/62 - 3/4/64
CDR C.E. Leighton, RCN — 3/4/64 - 6/12/66
CDR N. Brodeur RCN — 6/12/66 - 1/8/68
CDR J.M. Reid, RCN — 1/8/68 - 5/6/71
LCDR J. Bishop — 5/6/71 - 3/8/71
CDR L.A. Dzioba — 3/8/71 - 19/6/74
CDR J.B. O'Reilly — 19/6/74 - 8/1/76
CDR R.G. Balfour — 8/1/76 - 8/2/77
CDR C.J. Crow — 8/2/77 - 25/3/77
CDR R.G. Balfour — 25/3/77 - 29/7/77
CDR J.D. Large — 29/7/77 - 20/6/79
CDR J.K. Steele — 20/6/79 - 18/6/81
CDR G.J. Eldridge — 18/6/81 - 19/8/82
CDR D.R.E. Cooper — 19/8/82 - 30/7/84
CDR J.T. Jones — 30/7/84 - 5/5/86
CDR E.B. Waa — 15/5/86 - 21/4/88
CDR A.L. Vey — 21/4/88 - 28/9/89
CDR R.J. Neveu — 28/9/89 - 12/7/90
CDR S.D. Andrews — 12/7/90 - 2/7/91
CDR H.R. Smith — 2/7/91 - 19/7/93
CDR R.M. Williams — 19/7/93 - 14/7/95
CDR H.W. McEwen — 14/7/95 -

Toronto (2nd)

CDR R.D. Murphy 29/5/92 - 19/6/95
CDR L.J. Fleck 19/6/95 -

Vancouver (2nd)

CDR S.D. Andrews 2/7/91 - 31/3/93
CDR B.E. Matthews 31/3/93 - 28/7/95
CDR M.R. Bellows 28/7/95 -

Ville de Québec (2nd)

CDR J.J.P. Thiffault 4/9/92 - 7/7/95
CDR P.A. Guindon 7/7/95 -

Winnipeg (2nd)

CDR M.E.R. Brossard 10/6/94 -

Yukon

CDR R.W.J. Cocks, RCN 25/6/63 - 5/7/65
CDR R. Carle, RCN 5/7/65 - 1/9/66
CDR S.I. Ker, RCN 1/9/66 - 15/1/68
CDR P.G. May, RCN 15/1/68 - 12/9/69
CDR C.H.P. Shaw 12/9/69 - 28/6/71
LCDR D. Large 28/6/71 - 9/8/71
CDR C. Cotaras 9/8/71 - 9/8/73
CDR M.F. MacIntosh 9/8/73 - 1/10/76

CDR H. Kieran 1/10/76 - 15/5/78
CDR N.R. Boivin 15/5/78 - 22/5/81
CDR C.J. Crowe 22/5/81 - 25/7/83
CDR J.K. Steele 25/7/83 - 5/11/84
CDR M.F. Morres 5/11/84 - 23/4/86
CDR K.A. Nason 23/4/86 - 13/7/87
CDR K.V. Watson 13/7/87 - 31/7/89
CDR D.W. Fitzgerald 31/7/89 - 31/7/91
CDR J.G.V. Tremblay 31/7/91 - 31/7/92
CDR B.F. Lofthouse 31/7/92 - 30/7/93
CDR J.A.P. Lebel 30/7/93 - 3/12/93

Bibliography

Agnew, LCdr J., CAF. Navy Public Affairs, MARCOM, Halifax. Correspondence. June 1994.

Blakeney, Captain Darlene (ed). *Trident: The Newspaper of Maritime Command*. var. issues. Halifax.

Cline, Andrew. "HMCS *Mackenzie* Paid Off" in *Esprit de Corps, Canadian Military Then and Now*. January 1994.

Canada. Department of National Defence. Canadian Patrol Frigate Project - Navy Modernization. Ottawa: nd.

Canada. Department of Supply & Services. Canadian Patrol Frigate Project. 1991.

Canada's Navy, issues 1985-1990. Calgary: Corvus Publishing Group Ltd.

German, Cdr Tony, RCN (Rtd). *The Sea is at Our Gates: The History of the Canadian Navy*. Toronto: McClelland & Stewart, 1990.

Hobson, Sharon. *The Composition of Canada's Naval Fleet, 1946-85*. Halifax: Centre for Foreign Policy Studies, Dalhousie University, 1985.

Macgillivray, Captain Darroch, CAF (Rtd). In conversation. Halifax, NS, November 14, 1995.

MacKay, Ron. Canadian Coast Guard. In correspondence and conversation. Charlottetown, PEI. September, 1995.

Macpherson, Ken & John Burgess. *The Ships of Canada's Naval Forces, 1910-1993*. St. Catharines: Vanwell Publishing, 1993.

Quick, H.A., CAF (R). In conversation. Dartmouth, NS, 1994.

Saint John Shipbuilding Limited. In correspondence. Saint John, NB, 1993.

Sharpe, Captain Richard, OBE, RN (ed). *Jane's Fighting Ships*. var. ed. New York: Jane's Publishing Inc.

Sorsdahl, Captain N.R., HMCS *Saskatchewan*. In correspondence. March, 1994.

Timbrell, Rear-Admiral R.W., RCN (Rtd). In conversation. Dartmouth, NS, July 17,1995.

Tucker, Gilbert, PhD. *The Naval Service of Canada*. Vol.II. Ottawa: King's Printer, 1952.

Watts, Anthony J. (ed). "Canada Updates Navy", in *Navy International*. February,1981.

Photo Credits

(Negative numbers refer to Canadian Forces Photo)

Index of Ships